LIFE IN THE SPIRIT

LIFE IN THE SPIRIT

*Understanding the Gifts and Operation of the
Holy Spirit*

Dr. Charles Dixon

END TIME WAVE
PUBLICATIONS

Bogota, New Jersey

LIFE IN THE SPIRIT
Understanding the Gifts and Operation of the Holy Spirit

ISBN 1-889389-01-3

Note: In some Scripture quotations, italics have been added by the author for emphasis only.

Typesetter: Sheila Chang

TABLE OF CONTENTS

DEDICATION

I want to dedicate this book to my dear mother, Mary Tabi (Dixon), who was a single lady while raising me. You have done a great job and your imput has placed an everlasting mark upon my life. Thanks mom!

I also dedicate this book to those in the Body of Christ who have a passionate desire for the things of the Spirit.

ACKNOWLEDGEMENT

I want to thank Barbara Lyman for her continual support. I want to also urge you, the reader, to support her in her business endeavors. Ms. Lyman makes available superior products for food-stain removal from carpets and clothes. They work well on both white and color fabrics. You may contact her at:

Barbara Lyman
Mary Ellen Products
P.O. Box 39221
Edina, Minnisota 55439
(800) 328-6294

PREFACE

Now concerning spiritual gifts, brethren, I would not have you ignorant.
1 Corinthians 12:1

There is no force in all the world whose presence is so to be deplored as fear. Fear is destructive. Fears breeds suspicion, jealousy and hatred. It is fear which sets men (and nations) at variance. It is fear, nothing less, that has kept the world at war, and has hindered progress through the years.

In the spiritual realm, fear is our greatest foe, being Satan's most formidable weapon. Man, unsaved and unregenerated, is kept in bondage through fear of death.

The fear of man bringeth a snare: but whoso putteth his trust in the LORD
shall be safe.
Proverbs 29:25

In other words, fears hinders a Christian in his life of service unto his Lord; fear prevents many believers from going on in his Christian experience into the realm of the spirit.

THE BASIS OF ALL FEAR IS INGNORANCE

If the unsaved were not ignorant of the existence and plan of salvation, if they understood the significance and reality of the new birth, their fear of death would vanish. They would then be free to accept Christ and be saved. The same, in principle, applies to the Christian. When you, my Christian friend, receive enlightenment concerning the things of the Spirit, your fear of the supernatural will disappear, and as that fear goes it will be replaced by faith: faith in the things or God, faith in Christ Himself and faith in the things that pertain unto His Gospel.

It is made very clear by our text that we are to have a thorough and concise conception of spiritual gifts also. The gifts of the Spirit are not new. Nevertheless, the gifts of the Spirit in their fullest measure were to be the earmarks of the dispensation of grace, the age in which we live.

It is worth taking note of the fact that when Jesus commenced His ministry, He first read from Isaiah's prophecy.

Now who are we? What are we? Sinners, saved by the grace of God, that's all! Therefore if we are to do the works which He did, we shall have to have, and use, more - much more - than our natural abilities. This thought brings us back to our text, for the gifts of the Spirit are nothing more nor less than supernatural abilities, given of God, to us, that we might be made able to perform the works unto which we are called.

Therefore, if we would be wise, we should study the gifts of the Spirit and all available truth concerning them, their usage, etc., that we be not ignorant concerning them.

The gifts of the Spirit are nine in number; no more, no less. They are listed (by reference only) in the Word.

They are divided by their very nature, and the nature and characteristics of their operations, into three groups, with three gifts in each group. I have listed them in these groups, in their proper sequence, and under their respective headings. These headings are likewise suggested by the very nature and characteristics of the gifts and their operations.

INSPIRATIONAL, WORSHIP, OR UTTERANCE GIFTS:

1. The gift of Tongues.
2. The gift of the interpretation of Tongues
3. The gift of Prophecy.

REVELATION OR INSTRUCTIONAL GIFTS:

1. The gift of the word of knowledge.
2. The gift of the word of wisdom.
3. The gift of the discerning of spirits.

POWER OR IMPARTATION GIFTS:

1. The gift of faith.
2. The gift of healing
3. The gift of the performing of miracles.

INSPIRATIONAL, WORSHIP OR UTTERANCE GIFTS:

1. The gift of tongues is the God-given ability to speak in languages that you do not understand, and that at your own volition.

2. The gift of the interpretation of tongues is the God-given ability to bring forth in the language of your understanding, the sum and substance of that which has been spoken in another (to you unknown) tongue.

3. The gift of prophecy (the product of which constitute the testimony of Jesus) is the God-given ability to bring forth in the language of your understanding - but not via your understanding - a message direct from the heart of God to His people; a message that is always unto edification, exhortation and comfort; a message that always agrees with the Word of God.

These three gifts are referred to as utterance gifts because of their mode of operation. They are also referred to as worship gifts, because they are principally utilized in the worship of God. They are known as inspirational gifts because their use inspires both the user and them that hear.

REVELATION OR INSTRUCTIONAL GIFTS:

1. The gift of the word of knowledge is the God-given ability to take unto yourself, at your own volition, a word of knowledge (that is a revelation of facts concerning things about which it would be humanly impossible for you to know anything at all.)

2. The gift of the word of wisdom is the God-given ability to take unto yourself, at your own volition, a word of wisdom, this being a revelation of what to do about a situation once you know the facts concerning the case.

3. The gift of discerning of spirits is the God-given ability to detect the presence and acertain the identity of spirits to the end that, if evil, they may be cast out.

These three are referred to as revelation gifts because they operate by revelation only. They are also referred to as instructional gifts because of their use the child of God is instructed in his/her spiritual warfare.

POWER OR IMPARTATION GIFTS;

1. The gift of faith is the God-given ability to believe for the fantastically impossible to come to pass at your word, and to pass on, to instill, to inspire that faith in the hearts of others.

2. The gift of healing is the God-given ability to impart the healing virtue of Christ to another (provided they are in a position to receive).

3. The gift of the performing of miracles is the God-given ability to cause to come to pass acts that are contrary to, or beyond the realm of, the laws of nature.

These three are referred to as power gifts because they operate by the effectul working of that power which is in us, the power of God. They are called impartation gifts because by their use you impart something to others.
(All these supernatural abilities are operated entirely at your own will.)

Before we go on a step further, we would have you to understand fully the sigificance of the word "gift" as it is utilized with reference to these manifestations of the power and the Spirit of God.

The "gift" is the God-given ability to perform the act, the act differing in each case. For instance, in connection with the gift of tongues, the "gift" is the God-given ability to speak in other tongues at your own will; the act is the speaking in the said tongues. The same principle applies to all the gifts and to your receiving and operating of the same.

With these few thoughts in mind, let us commence our study of the gifts of the Spirit, knowing that we are in the will of God in doing so.

Dr. Charles Dixon
January 1997

THE GIFTS OF THE SPIRIT

PART ONE

THE UTTERANCE GIFTS OF THE SPIRIT

Know that the nine gifts of the Spirit divide automatically into three groups of three; that is, with each of the three groups consisting of three of the spiritual gifts.

It should be further noticed that these divisions are based upon the nature and characteristics of the gifts and the sequence or order of their operations.

The first of these groups, in order of operation, is the group known as the **utterance gifts.** This group is so named because the spiritual gifts which comprise it operate solely by utterance. Let's list them here in their proper order.

UTTERANCE GIFTS

1. **The Gift of Tongues**

2. **The Gift of the Interpretation of Tongues**

3. **The Gift of Prophecy**

Let's study them in that order.

CHAPTER ONE

THE GIFT OF TONGUES

I would that ye all spake with tongues...

I Corinthians 14:5A

WHAT IT IS NOT

The gift of tongues is not linguistic ability.

It is not the comprehension of languages.

It is not the ability to yell, scream or make hideous noises.

The things I have cited above is not the evidence of having received the Baptism of the Holy Spirit. But the latter is the evidence by speaking in other **tongues,** as the Spirit gives you utterance.

And they were all filled with the Holy Ghost, and began to speak with other tongues, as the Spirit gave them utterance.

Acts 2:4

And when Paul had laid his hands upon them, the Holy Ghost came on them; and they spake with tongues, and prophesied.

Acts 19:6

While Peter yet spake these words, the Holy Ghost fell on all them which heard the word.

And they of the circumcision which believed were astonished, as many as came with Peter, because that on the Gentiles also was poured out the gift of the Holy Ghost.

For they heard them speak with tongues, and magnify God. Then answered Peter,

Acts 10:44-46

WHAT IT IS

The gift of **tongues** is the God-given ability to speak in other **tongues** at will. That it is at your will is made evident by the rules and regulations in God's Word regarding its use. Nothing has brought more shame on the Church of Jesus

3

Christ than the much abuse of this gift. Many of the offenses were committed in ignorance. Please remember that our Father would not have us ignorant concerning these gifts.

> **Now concerning spiritual gifts, brethren, I would not have you ignorant.**
> **I Corinthians 12:1**

When we say that you speak in other **tongues,** we mean you speak with other **tongues** (languages) that you do not comprehend. Any language that you do not understand is another **tongue** to you. This is made very plain in the following references wherein the **tongue** spoken is referred to as "unknown."

> **For he that speaketh in an unknown tongue speaketh not unto men, but unto God: for no man understandeth him; howbeit in the spirit he speaketh mysteries.**
> **I Corinthians 14:2**

> **He that speaketh in an unknown tongue edifieth himself; but he that prophesieth edifieth the church.**
> **I Corinthians 14:4**

> **Wherefore let him that speaketh in an unknown tongue pray that he may interpret.**
> **I Corinthians 14:13**

> **For if I pray in an unknown tongue, my spirit prayeth, but my understanding is unfruitful.**
> **I Corinthians 14:14**

> **Yet in the church I had rather speak five words with my understanding, that by my voice I might teach others also, than ten thousand words in an unknown tongue.**
> **I Corinthians 14:19**

> **If any man speak in an unknown tongue, let it be by two, or at the most by three, and that by course; and let one interpret.**
> **I Corinthians 14:27**

This simply means that your understanding does not grasp the significance for the sounds that you utter.

> **For if I pray in an unknown tongue, my spirit prayeth, but my understanding is unfruitful.**
> **I Corinthians 14:14**

For he that speaketh in an unknown tongue speaketh not unto men, but unto God: for no man understandeth him; howbeit in the spirit he speaketh mysteries.

I Corinthians 14:2

I thank my God, I speak with tongues more than ye all:
I Corinthians 14:18

For if I pray in an unknown tongue, my spirit prayeth, but my understanding is unfruitful.

I Corinthians 14:14

This does away with any foolishness such as the so-called gift of languages as taught by some as special preparation for missionary service. Paul was the greatest of missionaries, yet the references make it plain that the **"other tongues"** he spoke were foreign to him and that he did not understand one word of that which he uttered at such times.

By natural linguistic ability, Paul spoke Greek.

And as Paul was to be led into the castle, he said unto the chief captain, May I speak unto thee? Who said, Canst thou speak Greek?

Art not thou that Egyptian, which before these days madest an uproar, and leddest out into the wilderness four thousand men that were murderers?

But Paul said, I am a man which am a Jew of Tarsus, a city in Cilicia, a citizen of no mean city: and, I beseech thee, suffer me to speak unto the people.
Acts 21:37-39

And when he had given him licence, Paul stood on the stairs, and beckoned with the hand unto the people. And when there was made a great silence, he spake unto them in the Hebrew tongue, saying,
Acts 21:40

This latter is not surprising, since Paul was a Hebrew; nevertheless, it was not the common language of the Hebrews of his day, but was reserved for the Temple worship. Hebrew and Greek were not **"other tongues"** to Paul.

WHAT THE GIFT OF TONGUES IS FOR

We should realize that there is plan and purpose in everything in which God engages. He does nothing in an abstract manner or without motive. This being so, it becomes evident that the gift of tongues is not given us without purpose. On the contrary, God has provided this supernatural ability with certain specific purposes and usages in mind. Now what are these?

First, the gift of **tongues** is to be utilized when talking to God.

For he that speaketh in an unknown tongue speaketh not unto men, but unto God: for no man understandeth him; howbeit in the spirit he speaketh mysteries.
I Corinthians 14:2

This is referred to by Paul as your spirit praying.

For if I pray in an unknown tongue, my spirit prayeth, but my understanding is unfruitful.
I Corinthians 14:14

Your understanding, he says, remains unfruitful.

...my understanding is unfruitful.
I Corinthians. 14:14B

The purpose behind this is to the end that you might edify yourself, build yourself up spiritually.

He that speaketh in an unknown tongue edifieth himself.
I Corinthians 14:14A

This gift, incidentally, is the only one whereby you may do this. Jude refers to this as building up yourselves on your most holy faith (Jude 20).

It produces this result in us largely by causing us to exercise faith. It requires a deliberate act of faith to speak in **tongues** unto God. However, there is a deeper significance. We are told that, when speaking to God in **tongues,** we are speaking in the spirit.

For he that speaketh in an unknown tongue speaketh not unto men, but unto God: for no man understandeth him; howbeit in the spirit he speaketh mysteries.
I Corinthians 14:2

Paul, referring to his own efforts in this regard, says:

...my spirit prayeth ....
I Corinthians 14:14

He declares, in effect, that this is speaking (or singing) with the spirit: that new spirit created within you by God at your conversion, i.e., when you were born again.

6

What is it then? I will pray with the spirit, and I will pray with the understanding also: I will sing with the spirit, and I will sing with the understanding also.
I Corinthians 14:15

There is a time to sing in other **tongues** and a time to sing in the language of your understanding. Paul states that when you give thanks in the spirit, you give thanks well.

Thou verily givest thanks well.
I Corinthians 14:17A

He makes it very clear, however, that no one else present understands you.

For he that speaketh in an unknown tongue speaketh not unto men, but unto God: for no man understandeth him; howbeit in the spirit he speaketh mysteries.
I Corinthians 14:2

He makes it very plain that it is your spirit that prayeth.

For if I pray in an unknown tongue, my spirit prayeth...
I Corinthians 14:14A

He makes it perfectly clear that he is not referring to the spirit of man which is in every man, but rather to the new man which is born of God.

Ye have received the Spirit of adoption, whereby we cry, Abba, Father.
Romans 8:15B

He reminds us that the spirit itself beareth witness with our spirit.
Romans 8:16

The Spirit likewise helps us by making intercession for us.

Likewise the Spirit also helpeth our infirmities: for we know not what we should pray for as we ought: but the Spirit itself maketh intercession for us with groanings which cannot be uttered.
Romans 8:26

This intercession is always according to the will of God.

And he that searcheth the hearts knoweth what is the mind of the Spirit, because he maketh intercession for the saints according to the will of God.
Romans 8:27

The speaking in **tongues** unto God strengthens you with might by His Spirit within you.

Strengthened with might by his Spirit in the inner man.
Ephesians 3:16B

The inner man is the new man or new creature.

Therefore if any man be in Christ, he is a new creature: old things are passed away; behold, all things are become new.
II Corinthians 5:17

The natural man, you see, can pray out of the will of God. It is possible for our understanding to clutter up the way. When we pray in **tongues** we pray according to the will of God, our understanding being laid temporarily to one side.

...my understanding is unfruitful.
I Corinthians 14:14B

Many folks wait for the urging of the Spirit to speak in **tongues**. This is not right, especially in connection with your speaking to God. This has to do with speaking for God, which we shall deal with next.

Please remember that you can deliberately speak to God in **tongues** any time you have received the gift of **tongues**. It is given for this express purpose, that you may edify yourself, build yourself up, in the spirit or strengthen yourself in the spiritual realm.

He that speaketh in an unknown tongue edifieth himself.
I Corinthians 14:14A

Second, the gift of **tongues** is for the purpose of bringing messages from God to His people. Unless there is interpretation, this is not fruitful, and is prohibited after the second, or at most the third attempt.

In other words, if a person utilizing the gift of **tongues,** and thus having brought forth a message from God to His people, fails to bring forth the interpretation of the message, it is permissible for that person to bring the message again in another **tongue.**

If there is still no interpretation, the person may be allowed to bring the message in yet another. If there is still no interpretation, the person may be allowed to bring the message yet in another **tongue.**

However, if at the conclusion of this third attempt there is still no interpretation, the person is to abstain from speaking in other tongues for the time being. This situation need never arise, however, for all may receive and utilize the gift of the interpretation of **tongues.**

This is the privilege of all believers who have received the baptism of the Holy Spirit and the gift of tongues. Here again many make the same error as in speaking to God: they wait for an urge; they expect the Lord to force them to bring a message. While it is true that without the inspiration of the Almighty a message in other tongues lacks flavor, please remember that the inspiration is within you.

If you will launch out in faith, commence to speak that message with tongues, the inspiration will be there. It is still you who does the speaking, and that at your will.

NOTE THE FOLLOWING REFERENCES

He that speaketh in an unknown tongue...
I Corinthians 14:2A

He that speaketh in an unknown tongue edifieth himself...
I Corinthians 14:4A

I would that ye all spake with tongues...
I Corinthians 14:5A

Paul speaking: ...I pray in an unknown tongue...
I Corinthians 14:14A

Again, Paul speaking:

I thank my God, I speak with tongues...
I Corinthians14:18

These and many more references make it plain that it is the person who does the speaking with tongues.

Speaking in other tongues, as a phenomenon of the Church Age, was foretold centuries before Christ by the prophet Isaiah.

For with stammering lips and another tongue will he speak to this people.
Isaiah 28:11

The prophet, incidentally, makes it very clear that the exercise of the gift of tongues, the actual speaking in other tongues, refreshes the soul of the speaker, and of them that hear him.

To whom he said, This is the rest wherewith ye may cause the weary to rest; and this is the refreshing.
                                        Isaiah 28:12

To refresh others by your deliberate operation of the gift of tongues necessitates your deliberate use of the gift of interpretation of tongues likewise, to the end that (the message being made intelligible to their understanding) they might receive the edification, and exhortation, and comfort our Lord desires they should receive. He intends for you, in this manner, to refresh the souls of men.

You refresh yourself supernaturally by speaking in tongues to God, thus making intercession in His will and receiving the benefits which He has ordained you to receive.

Speaking in tongues is a sign that shall follow believers.

And these signs shall follow them that believe ...they shall speak with new tongues.
                                        Mark 16:17

Tongues spoken are for a sign unto the unbelievers:

Wherefore tongues are for a sign...to them that believe not .
                                        I Corinthians 14:22A

They are not to be used in disorder, however, for if used so the unbeliever will be driven away.

If therefore the whole church be come together into one place, and all speak with tongues, and there come in those that are unlearned, or unbelievers, will they not say that ye are mad?
                                        I Corinthians 14:23

Tongues with interpretation of tongues equals prophecy, in that the Church of Jesus Christ is edified thereby.

He that speaketh in an unknown tongue edifieth himself; but he that prophesieth edifieth the church.

I would that ye all spake with tongues, but rather that ye prophesied: for greater is he that prophesieth than he that speaketh with tongues, except he interpret, that the church may receive edifying.
                                        I Corinthians 14:4-5

But if there be no interpreter, let him keep silence in the church; and let him speak to himself, and to God.
                                        I Corinthians 14:28

And the spirits of the prophets are subject to the prophets.
I Corinthians 14:32

For God is not the author of confusion, but of peace, as in all churches of
the saints.
I Corinthians 14:33

If any man speak in an unknown tongue, let it be by two, or at the most by
three, and that by course; and let one interpret.
I Corinthians 14:27

Let all things be done decently and in order.
I Corinthians 14:40

Do all speak with tongues?
I Corinthians 12:30

Many seem to interpret this as a statement of fact, which it is not; rather the
question is asked. All may speak with tongues; all should. It is the will of God for
all believers .

I would that ye all spake with tongues.
I Corinthians 14:5

People who mock the speaking in tongues and call it gibberish, show their
gross ignorance. No language is gibberish, though the tongue of the people may
sound very odd in the ears of a people of a different tongue.

There are, it may be, so many kinds of voices in the world, and none of
them is without signification.

There are, it may be, so many kinds of voices in the world, and none of
them is without signification.

Therefore if I know not the meaning of the voice, I shall be unto him that
speaketh a barbarian, and he that speaketh shall be a barbarian unto me.
I Corinthians 14:10-11

Many oppose speaking in tongues on the basis of "tongues shall cease"

... whether there be tongues, they shall cease. ..
I Corinthians 13:8

Correct! — But when? — When Jesus comes for us! But when that which
is perfect is come, then that which is in part shall be done away. 1Cor. 13:10

Study the context carefully: *now darkly, then face to face: now understand in part, prophesy in part: then know as we are known.*

Charity never faileth: but whether there be prophecies, they shall fail, whether there be tongues, they shall cease; whether there be knowledge, it shall vanish away.

For we know in part, and we prophesy in part. But when that which is perfect is come, then that which is in part shall be done away...
I Corinthians 13:8-10

Beloved, now are we the sons of God, and it doth not yet appear what we shall be: but we know that, when he shall appear, we shall be like him; for we shall see him as he is.
I John 3:2

As for me, I will behold thy face in righteousness: I shall be satisfied, when I awake, with thy likeness.
Psalm 17:15

Spiritual gifts are the weapons of our warfare for the Church Age. When Jesus comes, said Church Age shall end; spiritual gifts shall then be a thing of the past.

Paul used the gift of tongues in abundant measure.

I thank my God, I speak with tongues more than ye all:
I Corinthians 14:18

He declares that, since you are eager to possess and manifest spiritual gifts, you should try to excel at edifying the Church.

Even so ye, forasmuch as ye are zealous of spiritual gifts, seek that ye may excel to the edifying of the church.
I Corinthians 14:12

This simply means to earnestly strive to be the very best one at building up the remainder of the congregation spiritually. You can lift no one higher than you have been lifted yourself.

The husbandman that laboureth must be first partaker of the fruits.
II Timothy 2:6

First, build yourself up, edify yourself, your soul, your inner man.

...building up yourselves on your most holy faith, praying in the Holy Ghost.
Jude 20

He that speaketh in an unknown tongue edifieth himself; but he that
prophesieth edifieth the church.
I Corinthians 14:4

Next, edify the Church. To fulfill this, the desire of the heart of our God in connection with your use of the gift of tongues, you will need the gift of the interpretation of tongues, and knowledge concerning its use.

... they shall speak with new tongues ...
Mark 16:17

CHAPTER TWO

THE GIFT OF THE INTERPRETATION OF TONGUES

Wherefore let him that speaketh in an unknown tongue pray that he may interpret.

I Corinthians 14:13

WHAT IT IS NOT

It is not the ability to understand that which has been spoken in another language or tongue.

Every Biblical reference to the speaking in tongues makes it plain that the tongue spoken is unknown. If the gift of the interpretation of tongues was the ability to understand what was spoken, then the tongue spoken would not be unknown.

It is not the gift of the "translation" of tongues; there is no such gift. That which is brought forth by its operation is an interpretation: the sum and substance; not a translation, which is a word for word rendition of that which has been given in another tongue.

It is not the gift of the interpretation of dreams. Dreams are interpreted by the operation of the revelation gifts of the Spirit.

It is not the gift of interpretation. There is no such gift. It is the gift of the interpretation of tongues, and of tongues only.

WHAT IT IS

It is the ability given of God to bring forth, in your own language, the gist of what has just come forth in another tongue, whether that message in tongues came via your lips or those of another in the congregation.

A proper understanding of this truth will prevent a great deal of confusion.

It is an inspirational gift. That which you bring forth by its use is an inspired utterance. Speaking thus, you do not know what word you will utter next. It is given as you are inspired. This does away with the claims made by some people, such as, "I always have the interpretation, you know, though I don't always give it forth," or "I am sure Mrs. So-and-so did not give the right interpretation.

I had it all the time, though I didn't give it forth." These are ranks falsehoods and can easily be detected as such as we remember that it (the interpretation) is inspired utterance. The interpretation is not received by revelation. You speak as you are moved by the Spirit of God.

In other words, the interpretation is not in existence until it is uttered.

The gift of interpretation of tongues, like the gift of tongues, is entirely supernatural in its operation. That is the person speaking by the operation of the gift of interpretation of tongues is not actually interpreting, but rather is bringing forth — giving birth to — the interpretation.

Literally, to interpret from one tongue to another demands that the person interpreting understands both languages, the one in which the original message has been spoken and the one into which it is to be interpreted.

When a person, by the operation of the gift of the interpretation of tongues, brings forth the interpretation of a message that has been spoken in another tongue, that person is giving forth in the language of his understanding the sum and substance of that which has been spoken in a language he did not understand.

In fact, it is highly probable he did not even know in what language the said message was spoken: this is supernatural indeed

You who have the gift of tongues are under obligation to pray for the interpretation when you have brought a message in tongues in public.

Wherefore let him that speaketh in an unknown tongue pray that he may interpret.
I Corinthians 14:13

If any man speak in an unknown tongue, let it be by two, or at the most by three, and that by course; and let one interpret.

But if there be no interpreter, let him keep silence in the church; and let him speak to himself, and to God.
I Corinthians 14:27-28

This latter reference teaches us that if, after bringing a message in two or at the most three diverse tongues, there has been no interpretation given, the speaker is to be quiet, he is to keep silence, speaking to himself and to God.

Please note that this is a command of God.

If any man think himself to be a prophet, or spiritual, let him acknowledge that the things that I write unto you are the commandments of the Lord.
I Corinthians 14:37

A message spoken in another tongue with the interpretation equals prophecy in its ministry of edifying the Church.

I would that ye all spake with tongues, but rather that ye prophesied: for greater is he that prophesieth than he that speaketh with tongues, except he interpret, that the church may receive edifying.
I Corinthians 14:5

It is God's purpose in bestowing the gift of the interpretation of tongues upon His people, that by its use messages in tongues might be interpreted, thus making them understandable to the hearers.

The gift of interpretation of tongues is for all who have the gift of tongues.

I would that ye all spake with tongues, but rather that ye prophesied: for greater is he that prophesieth than he that speaketh with tongues, except he interpret, that the church may receive edifying.
I Corinthians 14:5

Wherefore, brethren, covet to prophesy, and forbid not to speak with tongues.
I Corinthians 14:39

But if there be no interpreter, let him keep silence in the church; and let him speak to himself, and to God.
I Corinthians 14:28

Wherefore let him that speaketh in an unknown tongue pray that he may interpret.
I Corinthians 14:13

It is senseless to pray for the interpretation unless you can interpret, that is, unless you have the gift and know-how to use it. God is consistent. He must have intended that all who have received the gift of tongues receive also the gift of the interpretation of tongues; and in effect His Word declares this to be so.

The Word of God is still the will of God. It is evidently His will that all believers should speak with tongues.

I would that ye all spake with tongues, but rather that ye prophesied: for greater is he that prophesieth than he that speaketh with tongues, except he interpret, that the church may receive edifying.
I Corinthians 14:5

It is just as evidently His will that all who do speak with tongues should interpret.

Wherefore let him that speaketh in an unknown tongue pray that he may interpret.
I Corinthians 14:13

Even so ye, forasmuch as ye are zealous of spiritual gifts, seek that ye may excel to the edifying of the church.
I Corinthians 14:12

Wherefore let him that speaketh in an unknown tongue pray that he may interpret.
I Corinthians 14:13

I would that ye all spake with tongues, but rather that ye prophesied: for greater is he that prophesieth than he that speaketh with tongues, except he interpret, that the church may receive edifying.
I Corinthians 14:5

CHAPTER THREE

THE GIFT OF PROPHECY

For ye may all prophesy one by one, that all may learn, and all may be comforted.
I Corinthians 14:31

WHAT IT IS NOT

The gift of prophecy is not the ability to preach.

Preaching is the art of public discoursing on the Scriptures.

It is not the art of **soothsaying**, i.e., fortune-telling.

It is not the ability to blast the saints. When a person, purporting to be utilizing the gift of prophecy, abuses the people of God, pronouncing wrath upon them, threatening them, etc., he is not prophesying.

Such a one is merely speaking presumptuously: his personal feelings are being relieved, his utterances are the perilous fruit of the meanings of his own mind directed by his erroneous doctrines.

WHAT IT IS

The gift of prophecy is the God-given ability to give forth in the language of your understanding a message direct from the heart of God to the hearts of His people; a message which is born as it is uttered — not premeditated; a message of edification unto His Church.

But he that prophesieth speaketh unto men to edification, and exhortation, and comfort.
I Corinthians 14:3

He that speaketh in an unknown tongue edifieth himself; but he that prophesieth edifieth the church.
I Corinthians 14:4

Remember that in this, as well as in the former utterance gifts, the gift is the God-given ability to perform the act, the act differing in the operation of each gift. This being so, we would ask, "what is the act in the operation of the gift of tongues?"

It is simply speaking language which you do not understand. What is the act in the operation of the gift of the interpretation of tongues? It is the giving forth,

19

in the language you ordinarily speak, the gist of what has gone forth in another tongue, a tongue you did not understand.

What is the act in the operation of the gift of prophecy? It is the giving forth in the language of the speaker, by inspiration, and entirely without premeditation, a message right from the heart of God. This gift operates by inspiration, not revelation. You do not know the message ahead of time. Such claims are falsehoods. Your prophetic utterances are not premeditated neither are they the meanderings of your own mind.

Herein lies the road to fanaticism. The gift of prophecy is an inspirational gift, a worship gift of utterance, not a revelation gift, not an avenue whereby you may claim for yourself or others the things you wish you or they possessed, not an outlet for the secret plans and ambitions of your heart.

True prophecy, the product of the operation of the gift, runs parallel to the Scriptures, sometimes consisting entirely of portions of the same. It is always unto *edification, exhortation and comfort.*

But he that prophesieth speaketh unto men to edification, and exhortation, and comfort.
I Corinthians 14:3

To **EDIFY** is to build up, to strengthen. Anything that tends to edify is unto edification. To **EXHORT** is to incite to a more worthy cause, to lovingly encourage to a more noble endeavor. Anything that tends to produce this effect is unto **EXHORTATION**. To **COMFORT** is to console, to inspirate. It also signifies a state of quiet enjoyment, of consolation. Anything that tends to bring us into such a state is unto comfort.

In this connection I will like to draw your attention to the visitation of the archangel Gabriel to Zacharias as he ministered in the temple.

And there appeared unto him an angel of the Lord standing on the right side of the altar of incense.

And when Zacharias saw him, he was troubled, and fear fell upon him.

But the angel said unto him, Fear not, Zacharias: for thy prayer is heard; and thy wife Elisabeth shall bear thee a son, and thou shalt call his name John.

And thou shalt have joy and gladness; and many shall rejoice at his birth.

For he shall be great in the sight of the Lord, and shall drink neither wine nor strong drink; and he shall be filled with the Holy Ghost, even from his mother's womb.

And many of the children of Israel shall he turn to the Lord their God.

And he shall go before him in the spirit and power of Elias, to turn the hearts of the fathers to the children, and the disobedient to the wisdom of the just; to make ready a people prepared for the Lord.
Luke 1:11-17

With the sudden appearance of the angel Gabriel, Zacharias was troubled and afraid — quite naturally so; and do not attempt to say you would not be. However, there is no word of rebuke from the lips of the messenger of the Almighty. "Fear not" said Gabriel — a messenger of comfort. Truly inspired utterance is earmarked here. When you hear a person prophesying — and saying, "Why are you afraid?" or "You're always afraid," or "My people are a fearful people. Why don't you walk with me? Stop being fearful!" etc. You know that someone is mixing the message with a bit of the natural mind, which is enmity with God.

God always comforts His people. He may speak in wrath to the unbeliever, but to His own His message is a loving, "Fear not."

Zacharias had been praying for the people. The next portion of the message assured him that his prayer was answered.

Now comes the big news. He is an old man. His wife is a barren woman, and now past the age of bearing. But the message of the Almighty declares that she shall bear him a son. Notice, not just a child, but the fact that it shall be a male child is disclosed, and he is given a name. The inspired utterances of God's people are just that positive. The balance of the message makes manifest God's plan and purpose for the life of this miracle — child by declaring in a positive manner the type of child he shall be, his ministry, and that which he shall accomplish therein.

Incidentally, all this transpired before there was conception in the womb, as the Scriptures declare.

And it came to pass, that, as soon as the days of his ministration were accomplished, he departed to his own house.

And after those days his wife Elisabeth conceived, and hid herself five months, saying,

Thus hath the Lord dealt with me in the days wherein he looked on me, to take away my reproach among men.
Luke 1:23-25

21

I would draw your attention next to Gabriel's visit to Mary.

And in the sixth month the angel Gabriel was sent from God unto a city of Galilee, named Nazareth,

To a virgin espoused to a man whose name was Joseph, of the house of David; and the virgin's name was Mary.

And the angel came in unto her, and said, Hail, thou that art highly favoured, the Lord is with thee: blessed art thou among women.

And when she saw him, she was troubled at his saying, and cast in her mind what manner of salutation this should be.

And the angel said unto her, Fear not, Mary: for thou hast found favour with God.

And, behold, thou shalt conceive in thy womb, and bring forth a son, and shalt call his name JESUS.

He shall be great, and shall be called the Son of the Highest: and the Lord God shall give unto him the throne of his father David:

And he shall reign over the house of Jacob for ever; and of his kingdom there shall be no end.

Then said Mary unto the angel, How shall this be, seeing I know not a man?

And the angel answered and said unto her, The Holy Ghost shall come upon thee, and the power of the Highest shall overshadow thee: therefore also that holy thing which shall be born of thee shall be called the Son of God.

And, behold, thy cousin Elisabeth, she hath also conceived a son in her old age: and this is the sixth month with her, who was called barren.

For with God nothing shall be impossible.

And Mary said, Behold the handmaid of the Lord; be it unto me according to thy word. And the angel departed from her.

Luke 1:26-38

Now let us review the entire incident. Here, as in the case of Zacharias, we find that which is natural: Mary is troubled at Gabriel's saying, his salutation. She is immediately comforted.

And the angel said unto her, Fear not, Mary: for thou hast found favour with God.
Luke 1:30

Now comes the big news, the heart and core of the message. It is rather a big order. Can she measure up to it? She is a devout Hebrew maiden; a virgin, and already espoused (promised in marriage) to a man named Joseph. To be found with child before they came together would be difficult to explain! Besides, a woman found in this fashion would be accused of having laid with some man, and be stoned to death; and who would believe her story? It was because Mary thought on all these things that she in finally asked the question:

Then said Mary unto the angel, How shall this be, seeing I know not a man?
Luke 1:34

How happy she would have been had the angel declared that the message referred to the first son she would bear to Joseph after their marriage! However, it was not so, and Gabriel assured her this was to be a virgin birth. God Himself would create the seed in the womb. She would be with child the usual period, nine months, and give birth to a fine baby boy without ever having known a man.

This was all very wonderful, but it still left her in the position where she might one day find herself standing before the council of chief priests and elders of Nazareth, with nothing wherewith to defend herself but her story of this unwitnessed meeting with Gabriel! Now she received the comfort, the edification, the exhortation she needed.

And, behold, thy cousin Elisabeth, she hath also conceived a son in her old age: and this is the sixth month with her, who was called barren.

For with God nothing shall be impossible.
Luke 1:36-37

That Mary now surrendered to the will of God is not to be wondered at, for she had been strengthened within by the words of the Lord, and she was now able to look the future full in the face with confidence that all would be well.

And Mary said, Behold the handmaid of the Lord; be it unto me according to thy word. And the angel departed from her.
Luke 1:38

And Mary arose in those days, and went into the hill country with haste, into a city of Juda;

And entered into the house of Zacharias, and saluted Elisabeth.
Luke 1:39-40

Here we find a perfectly normal reaction on the part of a normal, happy girl. She races to visit her cousin Elisabeth, eager to hear from her own lips all about this miracle — her being with child in her old age; she, who had been unfruitful throughout her proper years.

Only the Lord and Mary knew what went on in her heart and mind as she journeyed through the woodlands and meadows that day. What she said to Elisabeth concerning herself is as much a mystery. One thing is certain; before she had opportunity to tell one word of her secret — remember only she, and Gabriel, and the Lord knew anything about this matter — her cousin began to prophesy. And what a prophecy! It confirmed the message of the angel and established Mary's step in her walk of obedience to the will of God!

I would also remind you that Elisabeth was Hebrew, of the order of Aaron, the wife of a priest of Israel. This being so, much of the prophecy which went forth of her own mouth, did not agree with her teachings and traditions. To speak to her virgin cousin about "the fruit of her womb" was bad enough, but she must surely have wondered when she found herself saying:

And whence is this to me, that the mother of my Lord should come to me?
Luke 1:43

What do you say when your prophecy does not always necessarily agree with the language of your heart, your theologies, etc., but you can rest assured it will agree with the Word of God.

Now Mary prophesied:

And Mary said, My soul doth magnify the Lord,

And my spirit hath rejoiced in God my Saviour.

For he hath regarded the low estate of his handmaiden: for, behold, from henceforth all generations shall call me blessed.

For he that is mighty hath done to me great things; and holy is his name.

And his mercy is on them that fear him from generation to generation.

He hath shewed strength with his arm; he hath scattered the proud in the imagination of their hearts.

He hath put down the mighty from their seats, and exalted them of low degree.

He hath filled the hungry with good things; and the rich he hath sent empty away.

He hath holpen his servant Israel, in remembrance of his mercy;

As he spake to our fathers, to Abraham, and to his seed for ever.
Luke 1:46-55

Here again we find every indication that this is true prophecy, a fruit of her deliberate operation of the gift of prophecy.

Now Elisabeth's full time came that she should be delivered; and she brought forth a son.

And her neighbours and her cousins heard how the Lord had shewed great mercy upon her; and they rejoiced with her.

And it came to pass, that on the eighth day they came to circumcise the child; and they called him Zacharias, after the name of his father.

And his mother answered and said, Not so; but he shall be called John.

And they said unto her, There is none of thy kindred that is called by this name.
And they made signs to his father, how he would have him called.

And he asked for a writing table, and wrote, saying, His name is John. And they marvelled all.

And his mouth was opened immediately, and his tongue loosed, and he spake, and praised God.
Luke 1:57-64

Thus the prophecy concerning John was fulfilled, or at least a great portion of it was; and the rest was fulfilled later.

Now Zacharias prophesied:

And his father Zacharias was filled with the Holy Ghost, and prophesied, saying,

Blessed be the Lord God of Israel; for he hath visited and redeemed his people,

25

And hath raised up an horn of salvation for us in the house of his servant David;

As he spake by the mouth of his holy prophets, which have been since the world began:

That we should be saved from our enemies, and from the hand of all that hate us;

To perform the mercy promised to our fathers, and to remember his holy covenant;

The oath which he sware to our father Abraham,

That he would grant unto us, that we being delivered out of the hand of our enemies might serve him without fear,

In holiness and righteousness before him, all the days of our life.

And thou, child, shalt be called the prophet of the Highest: for thou shalt go before the face of the Lord to prepare his ways;

To give knowledge of salvation unto his people by the remission of their sins,

Through the tender mercy of our God; whereby the dayspring from on high hath visited us,

To give light to them that sit in darkness and in the shadow of death, to guide our feet into the way of peace.
                                                      Luke 1:67-79

In this amazing prophecy, he mentioned Christ as though He, who would not be born for another six months, was already born, had grown to manhood, had tasted death for every man, had ascended into heaven, and was now there meditating upon that which He had accomplished. John and his amazing ministry also received mention in this outstanding prophecy.

I would like to draw your attention to another very wonderful thought here. Can you place yourself, for a moment, in the shoes of either of John's parents? Do so; then read the prophecies relating to him. For purpose of illustration, read this one:

But the angel said unto him, Fear not, Zacharias: for thy prayer is heard; and thy wife Elisabeth shall bear thee a son, and thou shalt call his name John.

And thou shalt have joy and gladness; and many shall rejoice at his birth.

For he shall be great in the sight of the Lord, and shall drink neither wine nor strong drink; and he shall be filled with the Holy Ghost, even from his mother's womb.

And many of the children of Israel shall he turn to the Lord their God.

And he shall go before him in the spirit and power of Elias, to turn the hearts of the fathers to the children, and the disobedient to the wisdom of the just; to make ready a people prepared for the Lord.
Luke 1:13-17

Imagine the comfort John's parents received from this prophecy! No worry about their son. No fretting concerning his future. God had it planned! They had only to bring him up in the fear of the Lord. The rest would then follow in order. So, prophecy *edifies, exhorts and comforts* God's people.

Time passed. Eventually John was six months old.

And all went to be taxed, every one into his own city.

And Joseph also went up from Galilee, out of the city of Nazareth, into Judaea, unto the city of David, which is called Bethlehem; (because he was of the house and lineage of David:)

To be taxed with Mary his espoused wife, being great with child.

And so it was, that, while they were there, the days were accomplished that she should be delivered.

And she brought forth her firstborn son, and wrapped him in swaddling clothes, and laid him in a manger; because there was no room for them in the inn.

And there were in the same country shepherds abiding in the field, keeping watch over their flock by night.

And, lo, the angel of the Lord came upon them, and the glory of the Lord shone round about them: and they were sore afraid.

And the angel said unto them, Fear not: for, behold, I bring you good tidings of great joy, which shall be to all people.

For unto you is born this day in the city of David a Saviour, which is Christ the Lord.

And this shall be a sign unto you; Ye shall find the babe wrapped in swaddling clothes, lying in a manger.

And suddenly there was with the angel a multitude of the heavenly host praising God, and saying,

Glory to God in the highest, and on earth peace, good will toward men.
Luke 2:3-14

Note the message — the emphasized portions — and see for yourselves the earmarks of true prophecy here. But wait! Perhaps you think that, because angels brought this particular message, it is not prophecy! For that matter half the messages we have studied were brought by angelic messengers. I would simply ask you the following: Is not prophecy a message from the heart of God unto His people? Then does it matter who brings the message? Whether the message is delivered by an Angel, a man, a woman, or a child, is not the important thing. Neither will the message be altered because it is brought forth by this one or that one. Even a donkey prophesied to Balaam.

The message is the Lord's. It is the language and burden of His heart for His own, and as such it will bear the stamp of His handiwork. It will *edify, exhort and comfort* His people.

Shortly after Jesus was born, His parents journeyed to Jerusalem, there to present Him unto the Lord, and offer a sacrifice according to the law. The child was now in His fortieth day.

And, behold, there was a man in Jerusalem, whose name was Simeon; and the same man was just and devout, waiting for the consolation of Israel: and the Holy Ghost was upon him.

And it was revealed unto him by the Holy Ghost, that he should not see death, before he had seen the Lord's Christ.

And he came by the Spirit into the temple: and when the parents brought in the child Jesus, to do for him after the custom of the law,

Then took he him up in his arms, and blessed God, and said,

Lord, now lettest thou thy servant depart in peace, according to thy word:

For mine eyes have seen thy salvation,

Which thou hast prepared before the face of all people;

A light to lighten the Gentiles, and the glory of thy people Israel.
Luke 2:25-32

The older soldier of Zion had a further word which embraced the child's parents as well, for we read:

28

And Simeon blessed them, and said unto Mary his mother, Behold, this child is set for the fall and rising again of many in Israel; and for a sign which shall be spoken against;

(Yea, a sword shall pierce through thy own soul also,) that the thoughts of many hearts may be revealed.

Luke 2:34-35

Now I would ask you to read again, at your leisure, ALL the foregoing prophecies. You will discover that they ALL agree, the one with the other, that they complement each other; and that they ALL agree, are in harmony with, the Word of God. Inspired utterance never contradicts the Scriptures; true prophecy may even consist of portions of the Word. Above all else, it will always comfort, exhort and edify the people of God.

Regarding the literal aspect of the fulfillment of inspired utterances, we draw your attention to the prophecy of Joshua, when, after conquering Jericho, he prophesied concerning who would rebuild it.

And Joshua adjured them at that time, saying Cursed be the man before the LORD, that riseth up and buildeth this city Jericho: he shall lay the foundation therefore on his firstborn, and his youngest son shall he set up the gates of it.

Joshua 6:26

This prophecy was literally fulfilled centuries later.

In his days did Hiel the Bethelite build Jericho: he laid the foundation thereof in Abiram his firstborn, and set up the gates thereof in his youngest son Segub, according to the word of the LORD, which he spake by Joshua the son of Nun.

I Kings 16:34

Jesus prophesied concerning the gift of the Holy Spirit which they that believed on Him should afterwards receive.

In the last day, that great day of the feast, Jesus stood and cried, saying, If any man thirst, let him come unto me, and drink.

He that believeth on me, as the scripture hath said, out of his belly shall flow rivers of living water.

(But this spake he of the Spirit, which they that believe on him should receive: for the Holy Ghost was not yet given; because that Jesus was not yet glorified.)

John 7:37-39

This prophecy is literally fulfilled every time someone is baptized with the Holy Ghost.

29

And they were all filled with the Holy Ghost, and began to speak with other tongues, as the Spirit gave them utterance.
Acts 2:4

While Peter yet spake these words, the Holy Ghost fell on all them which heard the word.

And they of the circumcision which believed were astonished, as many as came with Peter, because that on the Gentiles also was poured out the gift of the Holy Ghost.

For they heard them speak with tongues, and magnify God. Then answered Peter,
Acts 10:44-46

And it came to pass, that, while Apollos was at Corinth, Paul having passed through the upper coasts came to Ephesus: and finding certain disciples,

He said unto them, Have ye received the Holy Ghost since ye believed? And they said unto him, We have not so much as heard whether there be any Holy Ghost.

And he said unto them, Unto what then were ye baptized? And they said, Unto John's baptism.

Then said Paul, John verily baptized with the baptism of repentance, saying unto the people, that they should believe on him which should come after him, that is, on Christ Jesus.

When they heard this, they were baptized in the name of the Lord Jesus.

And when Paul had laid his hands upon them, the Holy Ghost came on them; and they spake with tongues, and prophesied.
Acts 19:1-6

In each of the foregoing incidents you will notice that when the believers received the baptism with the Holy Spirt, something flowed out from their innermost being .

... out of the abundance of the heart the mouth speaketh.
Matthew 12:34B

In every case they spake with other tongues; fulfillment of Christ's prophecy concerning them which should receive His Spirit.

Besides the above and many other references in the Word, this prophecy of Jesus Christ's is literally fulfilled every time some believer receives the gift of the Holy Ghost.

With regard to the accuracy of inspired utterance, we draw your attention to Jude prophesying the fact that Enoch, the seventh from Adam, prophesied.

And Enoch also, the seventh from Adam, prophesied of these, saying, Behold, the Lord cometh with ten thousands of his saints,
Jude 14

This in itself is marvelous when we consider that almost four thousand years had passed into eternity since Enoch had prophesied, and that there was no written record of the fact he had prophesied, nor of the content of his prophecy. However, Jude not only prophesied that fact that Enoch had prophesied. By the operation of this mighty gift he also prophesied the very prophecy that Enoch had prophesied!

And Enoch also, the seventh from Adam, prophesied of these, saying, Behold, the Lord cometh with ten thousands of his saints,

To execute judgment upon all, and to convince all that are ungodly among them of all their ungodly deeds which they have ungodly committed, and of all their hard speeches which ungodly sinners have spoken against him.
Jude 14-15

I would like to share a few cases where God caused me to prophesy into the lives of individuals, and where He, God honored it and brought it to pass in their lives.

Just this year, I was ministering in a church in Raliegh, NC when the Word of the Lord came to me concerning a certain man in attendance who was diagnosed with cancer. This man was receiving chemotherapy treatments and was told that he was unable to have children. The Word of the Lord that came unto me was, "You are now being healed by God and you can now have children." In six weeks after I delivered that Word, I received a report that that same man's wife had just conceived in her womb by him, after years and years of trying.

Another case that God used me to prophesy into someone's life was when I met a pastor from Dallas, Texas. The Word of the Lord that came to me was that this pastor was going through extreme ministerial problems and he was in need of a building and land. I prophesied it over him and in less then two months this same pastor received a large lot of land with a building suited for that land right on it! (I also have a habit of having those that the Word of the Lord comes to pass after a prophesy is given, to document it and send me the testimony for my proof.)

We are urged to earnestly desire to prophecy above all else.

... but rather that ye may prophesy.
I Corinthians 14:1B

... but rather that ye prophesied: for greater is he that prophesieth than he that speaketh with tongues, except he interpret, that the church may receive edifying.
I Corinthians 14:5

Wherefore, brethren, covet to prophesy, and forbid not to speak with tongues.
I Corinthians 14:39

Our Lord desires that we ALL prophesy.

For ye may all prophesy ...
I Corinthians 14:31

This is to be done decently, and in order, (I Cor. 14:40); One by one. (I Cor. 14:3A).

God's plan and purpose here is that in this manner ALL may receive instruction and comfort.

...that all may learn, and all may be comforted ....
I Corinthians 14:31

Prophecy serves to convict the unbelievers and the unlearned.

But if all prophesy, and there come in one that believeth not, or one unlearned, he is convinced of all, he is judged of all:

And thus are the secrets of his heart made manifest; and so falling down on his face he will worship God, and report that God is in you of a truth.
I Corinthians 14:24-25

"One who believes not" is, of course, a person who has never accepted Christ; one who is not born again.

"One unlearned" is a person who, although born again, has not learned to walk godly in this present world. It also includes the person who has not learned to walk in the use of spiritual gifts. Such a one's misdeeds (or lack, as the case may be) are made manifest by prophecy to the end that he might learn to walk with God, and in the use of spiritual abilities that thus he might be comforted.

Prophecy, above all else, is misunderstood by present-day leaders. Many rise up with satirical remarks, such as that in the New Testament days prophecy is not given in the first person. I would ask all such to read the following.

But Peter, standing up with the eleven, lifted up his voice, and said unto them, Ye men of Judaea, and all ye that dwell at Jerusalem, be this known unto you, and hearken to my words:

For these are not drunken, as ye suppose, seeing it is but the third hour of the day.

But this is that which was spoken by the prophet Joel;

And it shall come to pass in the last days, saith God, I will pour out of my Spirit upon all flesh: and your sons and your daughters shall prophesy, and your young men shall see visions, and your old men shall dream dreams:

And on my servants and on my handmaidens I will pour out in those days of my Spirit; and they shall prophesy:

And I will shew wonders in heaven above, and signs in the earth beneath; blood, and fire, and vapour of smoke:

The sun shall be turned into darkness, and the moon into blood, before that great and notable day of the Lord come:

And it shall come to pass, that whosoever shall call on the name of the Lord shall be saved.

Acts 2:14-21

Note especially,

I will pour out of my Spirit .....on my servants ... my handmaidens ...I will pour out ... of my Spirit

Acts 2:18

... I will shew wonders, etc.

Acts 2:19

Of course some will say that Peter was only quoting Joel's prophecy. For that matter, read Joel's prophecy.

And it shall come to pass afterward, that I will pour out my spirit upon all flesh; and your sons and your daughters shall prophesy, your old men shall dream dreams, your young men shall see visions:

And also upon the servants and upon the handmaids in those days will I pour out my spirit.

And I will shew wonders in the heavens and in the earth, blood, and fire, and pillars of smoke.

The sun shall be turned into darkness, and the moon into blood, before the great and the terrible day of the LORD come.

And it shall come to pass, that whosoever shall call on the name of the LORD shall be delivered: for in mount Zion and in Jerusalem shall be deliverance, as the LORD hath said, and in the remnant whom the LORD shall call.
Joel 2:28-32

Note the slight difference in the phraseology employed by these two men and you will realize that Peter was not repeating a memorized portion of the book of Joel, but was prophesying. By prophecy he not only brought forth the same message as Joel, but he interpreted it — brought forth the hidden significance of it — as well.

Peter was in Joppa at the house of Simon the tanner, receiving, via a remarkable vision, instruction from God regarding the fact that the gospel was for the Gentiles also. And we read:

While Peter thought on the vision, the Spirit said unto him, Behold, three men seek thee.

Arise therefore, and get thee down, and go with them, doubting nothing: for I have sent them.
Acts 10:19-20

How does the Spirit speak in the New Testament days? How has He spoken in former days? By inspired utterance. Note the following Scripture portions

... The Holy Ghost said, separate me Barnabas and Saul for the work whereunto I have called them
Acts 13:2

When the Jews rejected their message, Barnabas and Paul waxed bold and said they would turn to the Gentiles, declaring the Lord had thus commanded them, saying:

For so hath the Lord commanded us, saying, I have set thee to be a light of the Gentiles, that thou shouldest be for salvation unto the ends of the earth.
Acts 13:47

No wonder these men waxed bold. They knew their authority.

The prophecy of Agabus is also very interesting:

And as we tarried there many days, there came down from Judaea a certain prophet, named Agabus.

And when he was come unto us, he took Paul's girdle, and bound his own hands and feet, and said, Thus saith the Holy Ghost, So shall the Jews at Jerusalem bind the man that owneth this girdle, and shall deliver him into the hands of the Gentiles.

Acts 21:10-11

We could draw your attention to many more references in God's Word that proved this point. However, enough has been said to more than convince any but the willfully blind. Let those that will to be ignorant remain so.

But if any man be ignorant, let him be ignorant.

I Corinthians 14:38

Let us, however, not forget that we are not to be ignorant.

Now concerning spiritual gifts, brethren, I would not have you ignorant.

I Corinthians 12:1

The gift of prophecy played a very important part in the lives and ministries of the first Apostles, and of the believers and workers of the early Church. For example, study the life and ministry of Paul. His first healing and the receiving of the Baptism were implemented by the use of this gift, or the gift of tongues with the gift of the interpretation of tongues.

And there was a certain disciple at Damascus, named Ananias; and to him said the Lord in a vision, Ananias. And he said, Behold, I am here, Lord.

And the Lord said unto him, Arise, and go into the street which is called Straight, and enquire in the house of Judas for one called Saul, of Tarsus: for, behold, he prayeth,

And hath seen in a vision a man named Ananias coming in, and putting his hand on him, that he might receive his sight.

Then Ananias answered, Lord, I have heard by many of this man, how much evil he hath done to thy saints at Jerusalem:

And here he hath authority from the chief priests to bind all that call on thy name.

But the Lord said unto him, Go thy way: for he is a chosen vessel unto me, to bear my name before the Gentiles, and kings, and the children of Israel:

For I will shew him how great things he must suffer for my name's sake.

And Ananias went his way, and entered into the house; and putting his hands on him said, Brother Saul, the Lord, even Jesus, that appeared unto thee in the way as thou camest, hath sent me, that thou mightest receive thy sight, and be filled with the Holy Ghost.

And immediately there fell from his eyes as it had been scales: and he received sight forthwith, and arose, and was baptized.

And when he had received meat, he was strengthened. Then was Saul certain days with the disciples which were at Damascus.
Acts 9:10-19

Paul's choice of Timothy for the position of pastor of the church at Ephesus was based upon certain inspired utterances which had gone before over the young man. Concerning the fact that it was Paul himself who had placed Timothy in control of the church at Ephesus when he himself departed for other fields, we read:

As I besought thee to abide still at Ephesus, when I went into Macedonia, that thou mightest charge some that they teach no other doctrine,
I Timothy 1:3

As to this purpose in leaving him there, we read:

As I besought thee to abide still at Ephesus, when I went into Macedonia, that thou mightest charge some that they teach no other doctrine,

Neither give heed to fables and endless genealogies, which minister questions, rather than godly edifying which is in faith: so do.
I Timothy 1:3-4

This charge I commit unto thee, son Timothy, according to the prophecies which went before on thee, that thou by them mightest war a good warfare;

I Timothy 1:18

Neglect not the gift that is in thee, which was given thee by prophecy, with the laying on of the hands of the presbytery.
I Timothy 4:14

The context makes plain the fact that Paul is here referring to the **gift of the discerning of Spirit.** The entire chapter is devoted to warnings, prophecies regarding evil spirits and the fact that they would bring in diverse and devilish doctrines to turn men away from the truth. For this reason, Timothy was exhorted not to neglect a certain, specific gift which he had received, which had been declared "in him" by prophecy. Because of all this, the gift referred to could only be the **gift of the discerning of spirits.**

Paul wrote to Timothy a second time. In this letter he referred to another spiritual gift, this one being in him by the laying on of his (Paul's) own hands.

Wherefore I put thee in remembrance that thou stir up the gift of God, which is in thee by the putting on of my hands.
II Timothy 1:6

Here again, the nature of the gift is declared by the context.

When I call to remembrance the unfeigned faith that is in thee, which dwelt first in thy grandmother Lois, and thy mother Eunice; and I am persuaded that in thee also.
II Timothy 1:5

If common sense means anything at all, this gift could be none other than the gift of faith. As to the fact that prophecy had declared this gift in him, it is only logical to deduce that unless inspired utterance had declared it, while Paul's hand were laid upon him, Timothy would not have the foggiest idea what gift Paul was referring to; neither would any of the apostles, nor any one else.

Furthermore, Paul referred to "Prophecies," the plural rather than the singular. Besides, both epistles to Timothy bear out the fact that the larger share of his warfare at Ephesus would be one of the discerning of spirits, to the end that, if evil, they might be cast out: and the inculcating of faith into the hearts of men and women of God.

If Paul, great soldier of the cross that he was, was humble enough to bow to prophecy, so shall I. Incidentally, Timothy was to war a good warfare by those prophecies that had gone forth over him, especially those which referred to his ministry.

This charge I commit unto thee, son Timothy, according to the prophecies which went before on thee, that thou by them mightest war a good warfare;
I Timothy 1:18

No one need be fooled by premeditated utterances, pawned off as prophetic utterances; neither does one commit error unwittingly in this field. Balaam, when walking in disobedience to the revealed will of Almighty God, still had to admit:

... I cannot go beyond the commandment of the LORD, to do either good or bad of mine own mind; but what the LORD saith, that will I speak?
Numbers 24:13

Regarding the use of the gift of prophecy, or the use of the gift of tongues with the gift of the interpretation of tongues, this man teaches us much.

And Balaam answered and said unto the servants of Balak, If Balak would give me his house full of silver and gold, I cannot go beyond the word of the LORD my God, to do less or more.

Numbers 22:18

And Balaam said unto Balak, Lo, I am come unto thee: have I now any power at all to say any thing? The word that God putteth in my mouth, that shall I speak.

Numbers 22:38

And he answered and said, Must I not take heed to speak that which the LORD hath put in my mouth?

Numbers 23:12

But Balaam answered and said unto Balak, Told not I thee, saying, All that the LORD speaketh, that I must do?

Numbers 23:26

Every one of these references have to do with inspired utterances, the product of our deliberate operation of the utterance gift of the Spirit. Balaam was simply stating the fact that if he was to speak by the operation of the utterance gifts of the Spirit, it was impossible for him to introduce therein anything of his own mind. By the same token, if he would introduce something of himself into the message, he must of necessity cease to utilize the supernatural abilities and deliberately play the hypocrite, declaring his own thoughts and ideas.

The prophet of Judah who cried against the altar at Beth-el came out of Judah by the word of the Lord.

And, behold, there came a man of God out of Judah by the word of the LORD unto Bethel: and Jeroboam stood by the altar to burn incense.

I Kings 13:1

He performed his task by the Word of the Lord.

And he cried against the altar in the word of the LORD, and said, O altar, altar, thus saith the LORD; Behold, a child shall be born unto the house of David, Josiah by name; and upon thee shall he offer the priests of the high places that burn incense upon thee, and men's bones shall be burnt upon thee.

I Kings 13:2

"The word of the Lord," as the term is utilized here, signified inspired utterance: that which you produce by your deliberate operation of the utterance gifts of the Spirit.

On the basis of the inspired utterance which went forth, apparently out of his own mouth before he left Judah, he refused the king's hospitality.

And the king said unto the man of God, Come home with me, and refresh thyself, and I will give thee a reward.

And the man of God said unto the king, If thou wilt give me half thine house, I will not go in with thee, neither will I eat bread nor drink water in this place:

For so was it charged me by the word of the LORD, saying, Eat no bread, nor drink water, nor turn again by the same way that thou camest.

I Kings 13:7-9

Up till now, our young man has done well. He came out of Judah on the basis of an inspired utterance. He has performed the works which he was ordained of God to perform, this also by the deliberate use of these supernatural abilities. He has refused the king's hospitality because to accept it would be to disobey the message he received in prophecy.

Now there dwelt an old prophet in Bethel; and his sons came and told him all the works that the man of God had done that day in Bethel: the words which he had spoken unto the king, them they told also to their father.

I Kings 13:11

This old prophet, desiring fellowship, followed the young man, and, finding him resting along the way, he lied to him, thus to entice him to his house for food, rest and fellowship.

He said unto him, I am a prophet also as thou art; and an angel spake unto me by the word of the LORD, saying, Bring him back with thee into thine house, that he may eat bread and drink water. But he lied unto him.

I Kings 13:18

Eventually they were seated at meat together and it was here, while they were eating, that the old prophet brought forth inspired utterance, the Word of the Lord.

And it came to pass, as they sat at the table, that the word of the LORD came unto the prophet that brought him back:

And he cried unto the man of God that came from Judah, saying, Thus saith the LORD, Forasmuch as thou hast disobeyed the mouth of the LORD, and hast not kept the commandment which the LORD thy God commanded thee,

But camest back, and hast eaten bread and drunk water in the place, of the which the LORD did say to thee, Eat no bread, and drink no water; thy carcase shall not come unto the sepulchre of thy fathers.

I Kings 13:20-22

The context in fact speaks for itself, proving the truth of the inspired utterance.

And it came to pass, after he had eaten bread, and after he had drunk, that he saddled for him the ass, to wit, for the prophet whom he had brought back.

And when he was gone, a lion met him by the way, and slew him: and his carcase was cast in the way, and the ass stood by it, the lion also stood by the carcase.

And, behold, men passed by, and saw the carcase cast in the way, and the lion standing by the carcase: and they came and told it in the city where the old prophet dwelt.

And when the prophet that brought him back from the way heard thereof, he said, It is the man of God, who was disobedient unto the word of the LORD: therefore the LORD hath delivered him unto the lion, which hath torn him, and slain him, according to the word of the LORD, which he spake unto him.

And he spake to his sons, saying, Saddle me the ass. And they saddled him.

And he went and found his carcase cast in the way, and the ass and the lion standing by the carcase: the lion had not eaten the carcase, nor torn the ass.

And the prophet took up the carcase of the man of God, and laid it upon the ass, and brought it back: and the old prophet came to the city, to mourn and to bury him.

And he laid his carcase in his own grave; and they mourned over him, saying, Alas, my brother!

I Kings 13:23-30

Again the old prophet — who, when in conversation with the young man, had lied, and lied seriously, concerning spiritual things — exercised the gift of prophecy, giving commandment at the same time concerning his own burial.

And it came to pass, after he had buried him, that he spake to his sons, saying, When I am dead, then bury me in the sepulchre wherein the man of God is buried; lay my bones beside his bones:

For the saying which he cried by the word of the LORD against the altar in
Bethel, and against all the houses of the high places which are in the cities of
Samaria, shall surely come to pass.

I Kings 13:31-32

All this was fulfilled, as was the prophecy of the young prophet.

Many hundreds of years later a young king arose named Josiah, even as
the prophecy had declared. He, fulfilled the inspired utterance to the letter, cleansed
Israel of her iniquity, purging her places of idolatry and destroying her idols. Yet
even at the height of his holy wrath, whilst from the bones of men being consumed
on the broken down altar of Beth-el the smoke ascended into the heavens, he spared
the bones of these two men of God.

And the king commanded Hilkiah the high priest, and the priests of the second
order, and the keepers of the door, to bring forth out of the temple of the
LORD all the vessels that were made for Baal, and for the grove, and for all
the host of heaven: and he burned them without Jerusalem in the fields of
Kidron, and carried the ashes of them unto Bethel.

And he put down the idolatrous priests, whom the kings of Judah had
ordained to burn incense in the high places in the cities of Judah, and in the
places round about Jerusalem; them also that burned incense unto Baal, to the
sun, and to the moon, and to the planets, and to all the host of heaven.

And he brought out the grove from the house of the LORD, without
Jerusalem, unto the brook Kidron, and burned it at the brook Kidron, and
stamped it small to powder, and cast the powder thereof upon the graves of the
children of the people.

And he brake down the houses of the sodomites, that were by the house of the
LORD, where the women wove hangings for the grove.

And he brought all the priests out of the cities of Judah, and defiled the high
places where the priests had burned incense, from Geba to Beersheba, and
brake down the high places of the gates that were in the entering in of the gate
of Joshua the governor of the city, which were on a man's left hand at the gate
of the city.

Nevertheless the priests of the high places came not up to the altar of the
LORD in Jerusalem, but they did eat of the unleavened bread among their
brethren.

And he defiled Topheth, which is in the valley of the children of Hinnom, that
no man might make his son or his daughter to pass through the fire to Molech.

And he took away the horses that the kings of Judah had given to the sun, at
the entering in of the house of the LORD, by the chamber of Nathanmelech the

chamberlain, which was in the suburbs, and burned the chariots of the sun with fire.

And the altars that were on the top of the upper chamber of Ahaz, which the kings of Judah had made, and the altars which Manasseh had made in the two courts of the house of the LORD, did the king beat down, and brake them down from thence, and cast the dust of them into the brook Kidron.

And the high places that were before Jerusalem, which were on the right hand of the mount of corruption, which Solomon the king of Israel had builded for Ashtoreth the abomination of the Zidonians, and for Chemosh the abomination of the Moabites, and for Milcom the abomination of the children of Ammon, did the king defile.

And he brake in pieces the images, and cut down the groves, and filled their places with the bones of men.

II Kings 23:4-14

And the king commanded Hilkiah the high priest, and the priests of the second order, and the keepers of the door, to bring forth out of the temple of the LORD all the vessels that were made for Baal, and for the grove, and for all the host of heaven: and he burned them without Jerusalem in the fields of Kidron, and carried the ashes of them unto Bethel.

And he put down the idolatrous priests, whom the kings of Judah had ordained to burn incense in the high places in the cities of Judah, and in the places round about Jerusalem; them also that burned incense unto Baal, to the sun, and to the moon, and to the planets, and to all the host of heaven.

And he brought out the grove from the house of the LORD, without Jerusalem, unto the brook Kidron, and burned it at the brook Kidron, and stamped it small to powder, and cast the powder thereof upon the graves of the children of the people.

And he brake down the houses of the sodomites, that were by the house of the LORD, where the women wove hangings for the grove.

And he brought all the priests out of the cities of Judah, and defiled the high places where the priests had burned incense, from Geba to Beersheba, and brake down the high places of the gates that were in the entering in of the gate of Joshua the governor of the city, which were on a man's left hand at the gate of the city.

Nevertheless the priests of the high places came not up to the altar of the LORD in Jerusalem, but they did eat of the unleavened bread among their brethren.

And he defiled Topheth, which is in the valley of the children of Hinnom, that no man might make his son or his daughter to pass through the fire to Molech.

And he took away the horses that the kings of Judah had given to the sun, at the entering in of the house of the LORD, by the chamber of Nathanmelech the chamberlain, which was in the suburbs, and burned the chariots of the sun with fire.

And the altars that were on the top of the upper chamber of Ahaz, which the kings of Judah had made, and the altars which Manasseh had made in the two courts of the house of the LORD, did the king beat down, and brake them down from thence, and cast the dust of them into the brook Kidron.
And the high places that were before Jerusalem, which were on the right hand of the mount of corruption, which Solomon the king of Israel had builded for Ashtoreth the abomination of the Zidonians, and for Chemosh the abomination of the Moabites, and for Milcom the abomination of the children of Ammon, did the king defile.

And he brake in pieces the images, and cut down the groves, and filled their places with the bones of men.

Moreover the altar that was at Bethel, and the high place which Jeroboam the son of Nebat, who made Israel to sin, had made, both that altar and the high place he brake down, and burned the high place, and stamped it small to powder, and burned the grove.

And as Josiah turned himself, he spied the sepulchres that were there in the mount, and sent, and took the bones out of the sepulchres, and burned them upon the altar, and polluted it, according to the word of the LORD which the man of God proclaimed, who proclaimed these words.

Then he said, What title is that that I see? And the men of the city told him, It is the sepulchre of the man of God, which came from Judah, and proclaimed these things that thou hast done against the altar of Bethel.

And he said, Let him alone; let no man move his bones. So they let his bones alone, with the bones of the prophet that came out of Samaria.

And all the houses also of the high places that were in the cities of Samaria, which the kings of Israel had made to provoke the LORD to anger, Josiah took away, and did to them according to all the acts that he had done in Bethel.

And he slew all the priests of the high places that were there upon the altars, and burned men's bones upon them, and returned to Jerusalem.

II Kings 23:4-20

Any who prophesy the dictates of their own heart and mind do so deliberately, and are perfectly aware of what they are doing. Anyone who is beguiled by such so-called prophetic utterance is either wilfully beguiled or else taken unawares in ignorance. Please remember that God does not want us to be ignorant of these things.

Now concerning spiritual gifts, brethren, I would not have you ignorant.

I Corinthians 12:1

The gift of prophecy has been horribly abused. It is not given to us to be used as the gypsy fortune-tellers use in divination. It is not for the handing out of personal leadings — who you are to marry, when to fast, etc. — as though the one possessing the gift were a mediator.

I personally have the privilege of laying my hands upon some thousands of believers during the course of my ministry, and have prophesied over a great many of them at such times, as I have been inspired of the Lord. In ministering to the sick, we are often detained momentarily by the spirit, to utter a word of prophecy, or tongues with interpretation, which equal prophecy. Then there is the laying on of hands for ordination to the ministry.

At a time like that, prophecy is definitely God's order, and this is what occurred in Timothy's case.

Neglect not the gift that is in thee, which was given thee by prophecy, with the laying on of the hands of the presbytery.
I Timothy 4:14

I have found that it pays to obey the Lord, and when He detains one and gives a word of utterance, not only is it in order to do so, but to disobey invites defeat. Besides, by failing to give forth inspired utterance at such a time, you also rob that saint of God's blessings needed at that particular moment.

To do so is the road of fanaticism. The beautiful gift of prophecy was not given to defile or to neglect, but to use for the glory of God. Let the gift of prophecy, be used for the things pertaining to the kingdom.

The gift of prophecy, like its companion gifts, the gift of tongues and the gift of the interpretation of tongues — is for all baptized believers; that is, all who have received the gift of the Holy Ghost.

For ye may all prophesy ...
I Corinthians 14:31

Wherefore, brethren, covet to prophesy, and forbid not to speak with tongues...
I Corinthians 14:39

This therefore constitutes the will of God concerning His disposition of this gift unto His own people.

... covet to prophesy...

I Corinthians 14:39

For ye may all prophesy one by one ...

I Corinthians 14:31

He that prophesieth speaketh unto men to edification and exhortation and comfort.

I Corinthians 14:3

Let all things be done unto edifying.

I Corinthians 14:26

... he that prophesieth edifieth the church.
I Corinthians 14:4

PART TWO

THE REVELATION GIFTS OF THE SPIRIT

PRELIMINARY

We have just concluded a brief study of the three utterance gifts. These constitute the first of three groups into which the nine gifts of the Spirit automatically divide.

The second group, in order of operation, is of course that of the revelation gifts. These are three in number; I will list them here in their proper order.

REVELATION GIFTS

1.   **The gift of the Word of Knowledge**

2.   **The gift of the Word of Wisdom**

3.   **The gift of the Discerning of Spirits**

These three are referred to as **revelation** gifts, because they function by **revelation.** They are listed in the above order because of their nature and the characteristics of their operations. We will study them in that order.

However, before we commence, let us get the following data straight. No one has ever received or utilized the **revelation** gifts of the Spirit without first being baptized with the Holy Ghost and having received the utterance gifts of the Spirit.

Please do not misunderstand me. I am not saying that you have never received a **revelation** from God. You may have been shown many things by Him. Indeed, you would never have realized your lost estate had He not revealed it to you. For that matter, whatever knowledge of His Word you may have, you received by **revelation** from the Most High.

But we are not studying **revelations.** We are studying the **revelation** gifts of the Spirit; supernatural abilities. If we will bear this in mind, we shall experience little difficulty in deriving from our study that which God desires us to receive.

CHAPTER FOUR

THE GIFT OF THE WORD OF KNOWLEDGE

Apply ... thine ears to the words of knowledge

Proverbs 23:12

WHAT IT IS NOT:

It is not human knowledge sanctified.

It is not an increased capacity to acquire understanding, though one of the ways in which the gifts of the Spirit in operation in us benefit us is in the effect they have in enlightening the mind.

It is not the ability to study the Bible, nor is it the ability to go to Bible school and study the Bible to acquire Bible knowledge.

WHAT IT IS:

The gift of the **word of knowledge** is the God-given ability to take unto yourself, at will, a revelation of facts concerning something about which it would be humanly impossible for you to know anything at all. The revelation thus received constitutes a **word of knowledge**.

We see this gift in operation in the life and ministry of Joseph as he interprets the dreams of Pharaoh's butler and baker in the dungeons of Egypt.

And the chief butler told his dream to Joseph, and said to him, In my dream, behold, a vine was before me;

And in the vine were three branches: and it was as though it budded, and her blossoms shot forth; and the clusters thereof brought forth ripe grapes:

And Pharaoh's cup was in my hand: and I took the grapes, and pressed them into Pharaoh's cup, and I gave the cup into Pharaoh's hand.

And Joseph said unto him, This is the interpretation of it: The three branches are three days:

Yet within three days shall Pharaoh lift up thine head, and restore thee unto thy place: and thou shalt deliver Pharaoh's cup into his hand, after the former manner when thou wast his butler.
                                        Genesis 40:9-13

When the chief baker saw that the interpretation was good, he said unto Joseph, I also was in my dream, and, behold, I had three white baskets on my head:

And in the uppermost basket there was of all manner of bakemeats for Pharaoh; and the birds did eat them out of the basket upon my head.

And Joseph answered and said, This is the interpretation thereof: The three baskets are three days:

Yet within three days shall Pharaoh lift up thy head from off thee, and shall hang thee on a tree; and the birds shall eat thy flesh from off thee.
Genesis 40:16-19

That the interpretations were true the Word of God testifies.

And it came to pass the third day, which was Pharaoh's birthday, that he made a feast unto all his servants: and he lifted up the head of the chief butler and of the chief baker among his servants.

And he restored the chief butler unto his butlership again; and he gave the cup into Pharaoh's hand:

But he hanged the chief baker: as Joseph had interpreted to them.
Genesis 40:20-22

Since it was humanly impossible for Joseph to have the slightest inkling as to the future of these men, it becomes apparent that he interpreted the dreams by the use of the gift of the **word of knowledge.**

In the course of time, the Pharaoh of Egypt dreamed dreams which troubled him. The Pharaoh's double dream was of fat cattle devouring thin cattle and full ears of corn eating thin, scrawny ears. He could find no one capable of interpreting that which he had dreamed till Joseph was brought before him.

And Joseph said unto Pharaoh, The dream of Pharaoh is one: God hath shewed Pharaoh what he is about to do.

The seven good kine are seven years; and the seven good ears are seven years: the dream is one.

And the seven thin and ill favoured kine that came up after them are seven years; and the seven empty ears blasted with the east wind shall be seven years of famine.

This is the thing which I have spoken unto Pharaoh: What God is about to do he sheweth unto Pharaoh.

Behold, there come seven years of great plenty throughout all the land of Egypt:

And there shall arise after them seven years of famine; and all the plenty shall be forgotten in the land of Egypt; and the famine shall consume the land;

And the plenty shall not be known in the land by reason of that famine following; for it shall be very grievous.

And for that the dream was doubled unto Pharaoh twice; it is because the thing is established by God, and God will shortly bring it to pass.
Genesis 41:25-32

Again the veracity of the interpretation was borne out. The seven years of plenty followed by seven years of famine truly came upon the earth, an established fact of his story.

Perhaps in no other realm has there been as much damage done to the work of God as in the realm of dreams, visions in the night, and faulty interpretations thereof.

It is certain that Joseph could not have known the facts concerning the dreams of Pharaoh, their significance, etc., in no other way than by the use of the gift of the word of knowledge. Only by the operation of this God-given ability could he reach out into the unknown and take unto himself, at his own will, a **revelation** of the facts concerning the problems which confronted him.

Next we find Daniel utilizing this gift, and by its use not only interpreting a dream for the king, but telling him what he dreamt. This transpired in Babylon. Daniel was one of the Hebrew captives resident there. The king in question was Nebuchadnezzar. His spirit was troubled to know the significance of his dream, but he was in a dilemma, for he had forgotten what he had dreamt.

The king answered and said to Daniel, whose name was Belteshazzar, Art thou able to make known unto me the dream which I have seen, and the interpretation thereof?

Daniel answered in the presence of the king, and said, The secret which the king hath demanded cannot the wise men, the astrologers, the magicians, the soothsayers, shew unto the king;

But there is a God in heaven that revealeth secrets, and maketh known to the king Nebuchadnezzar what shall be in the latter days. Thy dream, and the visions of thy head upon thy bed, are these;

As for thee, O king, thy thoughts came into thy mind upon thy bed, what should come to pass hereafter: and he that revealeth secrets maketh known to thee what shall come to pass.

But as for me, this secret is not revealed to me for any wisdom that I have more than any living, but for their sakes that shall make known the interpretation to the king, and that thou mightest know the thoughts of thy heart.

Daniel 2:26-30

Thou, O king, sawest, and behold a great image. This great image, whose brightness was excellent, stood before thee; and the form thereof was terrible.

This image's head was of fine gold, his breast and his arms of silver, his belly and his thighs of brass,

His legs of iron, his feet part of iron and part of clay.

Thou sawest till that a stone was cut out without hands, which smote the image upon his feet that were of iron and clay, and brake them to pieces.

Then was the iron, the clay, the brass, the silver, and the gold, broken to pieces together, and became like the chaff of the summer threshingfloors; and the wind carried them away, that no place was found for them: and the stone that smote the image became a great mountain, and filled the whole earth.

Daniel 2:31-35

This is the dream; and we will tell the interpretation thereof before the king.

Thou, O king, art a king of kings: for the God of heaven hath given thee a kingdom, power, and strength, and glory.

And wheresoever the children of men dwell, the beasts of the field and the fowls of the heaven hath he given into thine hand, and hath made thee ruler over them all. Thou art this head of gold.

And after thee shall arise another kingdom inferior to thee, and another third kingdom of brass, which shall bear rule over all the earth.

And the fourth kingdom shall be strong as iron: forasmuch as iron breaketh in pieces and subdueth all things: and as iron that breaketh all these, shall it break in pieces and bruise.

And whereas thou sawest the feet and toes, part of potters' clay, and part of iron, the kingdom shall be divided; but there shall be in it of the strength of the iron, forasmuch as thou sawest the iron mixed with miry clay.

And as the toes of the feet were part of iron, and part of clay, so the kingdom shall be partly strong, and partly broken.

And whereas thou sawest iron mixed with miry clay, they shall mingle themselves with the seed of men: but they shall not cleave one to another, even as iron is not mixed with clay.

And in the days of these kings shall the God of heaven set up a kingdom, which shall never be destroyed: and the kingdom shall not be left to other people, but it shall break in pieces and consume all these kingdoms, and it shall stand for ever.

Forasmuch as thou sawest that the stone was cut out of the mountain without hands, and that it brake in pieces the iron, the brass, the clay, the silver, and the gold; the great God hath made known to the king what shall come to pass hereafter: and the dream is certain, and the interpretation thereof sure.
Daniel 2:36-45

When a person dreams, the image is projected upon the membranes of the brain within the cranial structure. One literally views his own private movies in "bone threatre." Not only so, but no one else in the whole wide world views it but them.

When we realize this, and the fact that the king Nebuchadnezzar had forgotten what he dreamed, we can readily see that only by the operation of the gift of the word of knowledge was Daniel made able to perform these mighty works:

1.   To tell the king what he dreamed.

2.   To tell him what the dream signified.

Notice also that Daniel knew — and he could only know this by revelation — that the king, ere he slept that memorable night, had for some time laid in bed thinking about what the future might hold for this old world. This is made plain by the following statement, addressed by Daniel to the king at that time.

As for thee, O king, thy thoughts came into thy mind upon thy bed, what should come to pass hereafter: and he that revealeth secrets maketh known to thee what shall come to pass.
Daniel 2:29

Years later, the king was again troubled by a dream of ill omen. All others failing, he turned once more to Daniel for the interpretation. The monarch himself relates the incident.

But at the last Daniel came in before me, whose name was Belteshazzar, according to the name of my god, and in whom is the spirit of the holy gods: and before him I told the dream, saying,

O Belteshazzar, master of the magicians, because I know that the spirit of the holy gods is in thee, and no secret troubleth thee, tell me the visions of my dream that I have seen, and the interpretation thereof.

Thus were the visions of mine head in my bed; I saw, and behold a tree in the midst of the earth, and the height thereof was great.

The tree grew, and was strong, and the height thereof reached unto heaven, and the sight thereof to the end of all the earth:

The leaves thereof were fair, and the fruit thereof much, and in it was meat for all: the beasts of the field had shadow under it, and the fowls of the heaven dwelt in the boughs thereof, and all flesh was fed of it.

I saw in the visions of my head upon my bed, and, behold, a watcher and an holy one came down from heaven;

He cried aloud, and said thus, Hew down the tree, and cut off his branches, shake off his leaves, and scatter his fruit: let the beasts get away from under it, and the fowls from his branches:

Nevertheless leave the stump of his roots in the earth, even with a band of iron and brass, in the tender grass of the field; and let it be wet with the dew of heaven, and let his portion be with the beasts in the grass of the earth:

Let his heart be changed from man's, and let a beast's heart be given unto him; and let seven times pass over him.

This matter is by the decree of the watchers, and the demand by the word of the holy ones: to the intent that the living may know that the most High ruleth in the kingdom of men, and giveth it to whomsoever he will, and setteth up over it the basest of men.

This dream I king Nebuchadnezzar have seen. Now thou, O Belteshazzar, declare the interpretation thereof, forasmuch as all the wise men of my kingdom are not able to make known unto me the interpretation: but thou art able; for the spirit of the holy gods is in thee.
Daniel 4:8-18

This latter verse manifests the fact that because of his former experience in this realm with him, the king expressed his confidence in Daniel's ability to solve this mystery. Daniel interpreted the dream for the king.

The tree that thou sawest, which grew, and was strong, whose height reached unto the heaven, and the sight thereof to all the earth;

Whose leaves were fair, and the fruit thereof much, and in it was meat for all; under which the beasts of the field dwelt, and upon whose branches the fowls of the heaven had their habitation:

It is thou, O king, that art grown and become strong: for thy greatness is grown, and reacheth unto heaven, and thy dominion to the end of the earth.

And whereas the king saw a watcher and an holy one coming down from heaven, and saying, Hew the tree down, and destroy it; yet leave the stump of the roots thereof in the earth, even with a band of iron and brass, in the tender grass of the field; and let it be wet with the dew of heaven, and let his portion be with the beasts of the field, till seven times pass over him;

This is the interpretation, O king, and this is the decree of the most High, which is come upon my lord the king:

That they shall drive thee from men, and thy dwelling shall be with the beasts of the field, and they shall make thee to eat grass as oxen, and they shall wet thee with the dew of heaven, and seven times shall pass over thee, till thou know that the most High ruleth in the kingdom of men, and giveth it to whomsoever he will.

And whereas they commanded to leave the stump of the tree roots; thy kingdom shall be sure unto thee, after that thou shalt have known that the heavens do rule.
Daniel 4:20-26

The fact that this was the true interpretation of the dream is apparent, for all this was fulfilled to the letter.

All this came upon the king Nebuchadnezzar.
Daniel 4:28

Samuel, one of God's greatest men, likewise walked in the use of the gift of the word of knowledge. In fact, his amazing ministry would have been impossible without the use of this supernatural ability. In three chapters of the Word, we read of his continued use of the utterance and revelation gifts of the Spirit in conjunction one with the other.

And it came to pass, when Samuel was old, that he made his sons judges over Israel.

Now the name of his firstborn was Joel; and the name of his second, Abiah: they were judges in Beersheba.

And his sons walked not in his ways, but turned aside after lucre, and took bribes, and perverted judgment.

Then all the elders of Israel gathered themselves together, and came to Samuel unto Ramah,

And said unto him, Behold, thou art old, and thy sons walk not in thy ways: now make us a king to judge us like all the nations.

But the thing displeased Samuel, when they said, Give us a king to judge us. And Samuel prayed unto the LORD.

I Samuel 8:1-6

And the LORD said unto Samuel,(here we have inspired utterance), Hearken unto the voice of the people in all that they say unto thee: for they have not rejected thee, but they have rejected me, that I should not reign over them.

According to all the works which they have done since the day that I brought them up out of Egypt even unto this day, wherewith they have forsaken me, and served other gods, so do they also unto thee.

Now therefore hearken unto their voice: howbeit yet protest solemnly unto them, and shew them the manner of the king that shall reign over them.

I Samuel 8:7-9

Next you will see the gift of the word of knowledge manifestly in operation in this man of God.

And he said, This will be the manner of the king that shall reign over you: He will take your sons, and appoint them for himself, for his chariots, and to be his horsemen; and some shall run before his chariots.

And he will appoint him captains over thousands, and captains over fifties; and will set them to ear his ground, and to reap his harvest, and to make his instruments of war, and instruments of his chariots.

And he will take your daughters to be confectionaries, and to be cooks, and to be bakers.

And he will take your fields, and your vineyards, and your oliveyards, even the best of them, and give them to his servants.

And he will take the tenth of your seed, and of your vineyards, and give to his officers, and to his servants.

And he will take your menservants, and your maidservants, and your goodliest young men, and your asses, and put them to his work.

He will take the tenth of your sheep: and ye shall be his servants.

And ye shall cry out in that day because of your king which ye shall have chosen you; and the LORD will not hear you in that day.
I Samuel 8:11-18

When you consider the fact that no one, not even Samuel, had the foggiest notion of who was to be king, let alone any knowledge of his character or governmental policies, it becomes evident that in declaring the foregoing the prophet was exercising the gift of the word of knowledge.

Again we read:

Now there was a man of Benjamin, whose name was Kish, the son of Abiel, the son of Zeror, the son of Bechorath, the son of Aphiah, a Benjamite, a mighty man of power.

And he had a son, whose name was Saul, a choice young man, and a goodly: and there was not among the children of Israel a goodlier person than he: from his shoulders and upward he was higher than any of the people.

And the asses of Kish Saul's father were lost. And Kish said to Saul his son, Take now one of the servants with thee, and arise, go seek the asses.

And he passed through mount Ephraim, and passed through the land of Shalisha, but they found them not: then they passed through the land of Shalim, and there they were not: and he passed through the land of the Benjamites, but they found them not.

And when they were come to the land of Zuph, Saul said to his servant that was with him, Come, and let us return; lest my father leave caring for the asses, and take thought for us.

And he said unto him, Behold now, there is in this city a man of God, and he is an honourable man; all that he saith cometh surely to pass: now let us go thither; peradventure he can shew us our way that we should go.
I Samuel 9:1-6

We will discover a bit further on in this chapter that these weary seekers-after-asses never asked Samuel to tell them where they might find the lost beasts. They never mentioned them. Peradventure, said the servant, and peradventure he meant.

And they went up into the city: and when they were come into the city, behold, Samuel came out against them, for to go up to the high place.

Now the LORD had told Samuel in his ear a day before Saul came, saying,

To morrow about this time I will send thee a man out of the land of Benjamin, and thou shalt anoint him to be captain over my people Israel, that he may

save my people out of the hand of the Philistines: for I have looked upon my people, because their cry is come unto me.

And when Samuel saw Saul, the LORD said unto him, Behold the man whom I spake to thee of! This same shall reign over my people.

Then Saul drew near to Samuel in the gate, and said, Tell me, I pray thee, where the seer's house is.

And Samuel answered Saul, and said, I am the seer: go up before me unto the high place; for ye shall eat with me to day, and to morrow I will let thee go, and will tell thee all that is in thine heart.

And as for thine asses that were lost three days ago, set not thy mind on them; for they are found. And on whom is all the desire of Israel? Is it not on thee, and on all thy father's house?
                                                    I Samuel 9:14-20

Here you have continual use of the utterance gifts of the Spirit in conjunction with the use of the gift of the word of knowledge. Did you notice the reference to the asses? There was only one way Samuel could have known of the lost asses and their fate; that is by the operation of the gift of the word of knowledge.

And Samuel took Saul and his servant, and brought them into the parlour, and made them sit in the chiefest place among them that were bidden, which were about thirty persons.

And Samuel said unto the cook, Bring the portion which I gave thee, of which I said unto thee, Set it by thee.

And the cook took up the shoulder, and that which was upon it, and set it before Saul. And Samuel said, Behold that which is left! Set it before thee, and eat: for unto this time hath it been kept for thee since I said, I have invited the people. So Saul did eat with Samuel that day.
                                                    I Samuel 9:22-24

And when they were come down from the high place into the city, Samuel communed with Saul upon the top of the house.

And they arose early: and it came to pass about the spring of the day, that Samuel called Saul to the top of the house, saying, Up, that I may send thee away. And Saul arose, and they went out both of them, he and Samuel, abroad.

And as they were going down to the end of the city, Samuel said to Saul, Bid the servant pass on before us, (and he passed on,) but stand thou still a while, that I may shew thee the word of God.
                                                    I Samuel 9:25-27

Then Samuel took a vial of oil, and poured it upon his head, and kissed him, and said, Is it not because the LORD hath anointed thee to be captain over his inheritance?

When thou art departed from me to day, then thou shalt find two men by Rachel's sepulchre in the border of Benjamin at Zelzah; and they will say unto thee, The asses which thou wentest to seek are found: and, lo, thy father hath left the care of the asses, and sorroweth for you, saying, What shall I do for my son?

Then shalt thou go on forward from thence, and thou shalt come to the plain of Tabor, and there shall meet thee three men going up to God to Bethel, one carrying three kids, and another carrying three loaves of bread, and another carrying a bottle of wine:

And they will salute thee, and give thee two loaves of bread; which thou shalt receive of their hands.

After that thou shalt come to the hill of God, where is the garrison of the Philistines: and it shall come to pass, when thou art come thither to the city, that thou shalt meet a company of prophets coming down from the high place with a psaltery, and a tabret, and a pipe, and a harp, before them; and they shall prophesy:

And the Spirit of the LORD will come upon thee, and thou shalt prophesy with them, and shalt be turned into another man.
I Samuel 10:1-6

In the foregoing, Samuel, via the operation of the gift of the word of knowledge, foretells those things which are to come to pass that day in the life of Saul. Please remember that Saul never asked for any of this. This is the big secret. Ask for it, and you give opportunity for the natural mind to enter the picture. Ask for it, and you open the door to fanaticism. Leave things alone and let the Spirit of God move on the heart of the man of God; if anything is to be revealed, it will be, and you will receive the benefit.

Incidentally, the gifts of the Spirit are not toys; neither does God move on the hearts of His servants to use them merely to satisfy the whims, the fancies, of His people. There is no plan and motive behind all the works of the most High. In the case of Saul, these things were all foretold to the end that his faith might be established, that it be rooted and grounded in the power of God.

Remember also that none of these events transpired because Samuel declared they would be. They would have come to pass anyway, but God was glorified inasmuch as it was He who had made His prophet able to foretell them. This fact itself should have had a stabilizing effect on Saul.

And let it be, when these signs are come unto thee, that thou do as occasion serve thee; for God is with thee.
I Samuel 10:7

It was not God's fault that Saul failed, nor was it Samuel's. His use of the gift of the word of knowledge in the handling of the whole affair should have sufficient in itself to encourage Saul to go forward in implicit obedience to God in spite of all the forces of men or devils.

One of the most dramatic of all references to the use of the gift of the word of knowledge is the following excerpt from the ministry of the aged prophet Ahijah. The incident referred to occurred during the reign of Jeroboam, the king of Israel.

At that time Abijah the son of Jeroboam fell sick.

And Jeroboam said to his wife, Arise, I pray thee, and disguise thyself, that thou be not known to be the wife of Jeroboam; and get thee to Shiloh: behold, there is Ahijah the prophet, which told me that I should be king over this people.

And take with thee ten loaves, and cracknels, and a cruse of honey, and go to him: he shall tell thee what shall become of the child.

And Jeroboam's wife did so, and arose, and went to Shiloh, and came to the house of Ahijah. But Ahijah could not see; for his eyes were set by reason of his age.
I Kings 14:1-4

And the LORD said unto Ahijah, Behold, the wife of Jeroboam cometh to ask a thing of thee for her son; for he is sick: thus and thus shalt thou say unto her: for it shall be, when she cometh in, that she shall feign herself to be another woman.

And it was so, when Ahijah heard the sound of her feet, as she came in at the door, that he said, Come in, thou wife of Jeroboam; why feignest thou thyself to be another? For I am sent to thee with heavy tidings.
I Kings 14:5-6

Ahijah could not have known that the one approaching his door was the queen, only by the use of the gift of the word of knowledge. As for her, she might have saved herself the trouble of disguising.

Here again we find utterance gifts utilized in conjunction with the gift of the word of knowledge, the marvelous God-given ability to take unto yourself, at will, a revelation of facts concerning something about which it would be humanly impossible for you to know anything at all.

But Gehazi, the servant of Elisha the man of God, said, Behold, my master hath spared Naaman this Syrian, in not receiving at his hands that which he brought: but, as the LORD liveth, I will run after him, and take somewhat of him.

So Gehazi followed after Naaman. And when Naaman saw him running after him, he lighted down from the chariot to meet him, and said, Is all well?

And he said, All is well. My master hath sent me, saying, Behold, even now there be come to me from mount Ephraim two young men of the sons of the prophets: give them, I pray thee, a talent of silver, and two changes of garments.

And Naaman said, Be content, take two talents. And he urged him, and bound two talents of silver in two bags, with two changes of garments, and laid them upon two of his servants; and they bare them before him.

And when he came to the tower, he took them from their hand, and bestowed them in the house: and he let the men go, and they departed.

But he went in, and stood before his master. And Elisha said unto him, Whence comest thou, Gehazi? And he said, Thy servant went no whither.

And he said unto him, Went not mine heart with thee, when the man turned again from his chariot to meet thee? Is it a time to receive money, and to receive garments, and oliveyards, and vineyards, and sheep, and oxen, and menservants, and maidservants?

The leprosy therefore of Naaman shall cleave unto thee, and unto thy seed for ever. And he went out from his presence a leper as white as snow.
II Kings 5:20-27

Not only did the prophet of God know (and how could he, but by the use of this supernatural ability?) all about Gehazi's meeting with Naaman on the highway, his receiving of goods, the lies he told there, his hiding of the goods and the cash he received, and his plans for the future.

He also knew and foretold the punishment which, in a moment, was due to fall upon him for this. Please remember also that Gehazi did not become a leper because Elisha declared he would be one; rather, the matter was foreknown and declared, thus glorifying the Lord.

The days came about when Syria was at war with Israel.

Then the king of Syria warred against Israel, and took counsel with his servants, saying, In such and such a place shall be my camp.

61

And the man of God sent unto the king of Israel, saying, Beware that thou pass not such a place; for thither the Syrians are come down.

And the king of Israel sent to the place which the man of God told him and warned him of, and saved himself there, not once nor twice.

Therefore the heart of the king of Syria was sore troubled for this thing; and he called his servants, and said unto them, Will ye not shew me which of us is for the king of Israel?

And one of his servants said, None, my lord, O king: but Elisha, the prophet that is in Israel, telleth the king of Israel the words that thou speakest in thy bedchamber.
II Kings 6:8-12

Samaria was the capital of Israel, situated deep in the interior of Palestine. Damascus was situated deep within the heart of Syria, and was the capital city thereof. Syria lies to the north-northeast of Palestine. With all those miles between these two cities, Elisha, who lived at Samaria, kept the king of Israel, who likewise dwelt there, informed concerning all the battle-plans, troop-movements, etc., of the opposing forces, even to the word relative to the same spoken in secret by the king of Syria in his bedroom! This he could only accomplish by his deliberate use of the gift of the word of knowledge.

When at a later date the king of Israel sought to slay Elisha, he knew of it aforehand, and acting upon the revelation, saved his own life. Blaming Elisha for the predicament of Samaria, the monarch raged against the prophet.

Then he said, God do so and more also to me, if the head of Elisha the son of Shaphat shall stand on him this day.

But Elisha sat in his house, and the elders sat with him; and the king sent a man from before him: but ere the messenger came to him, he said to the elders, See ye how this son of a murderer hath sent to take away mine head? Look, when the messenger cometh, shut the door, and hold him fast at the door: is not the sound of his master's feet behind him?

And while he yet talked with them, behold, the messenger came down unto him: and he said, Behold, this evil is of the LORD; what should I wait for the LORD any longer?
II Kings 6:31-33

The prophet of God now utilized the utterance gifts of the Spirit, declaring that in twenty four hours the famine-ridden city of Samaria would be overflowing with a superabundance of foodstuffs.

Then Elisha said, Hear ye the word of the LORD; Thus saith the LORD, To morrow about this time shall a measure of fine flour be sold for a shekel, and two measures of barley for a shekel, in the gate of Samaria.
II Kings 7:1

A noble who stood nearby scoffed at this inspired utterance.

Then a lord on whose hand the king leaned answered the man of God, and said, Behold, if the LORD would make windows in heaven, might this thing be? And he said, Behold, thou shalt see it with thine eyes, but shalt not eat thereof.
II Kings 7:2

Whereupon Elisha declared the following revelation:

Behold, thou shalt see it with thine eyes, but shalt not eat thereof...
II Kings 7:2B

Foodstuffs arrived. The people flocked out to secure them, and to bring them through the gates into the city. The king appointed this same man to oversee matters at the gates, and we read:

And the king appointed the lord on whose hand he leaned to have the charge of the gate: and the people trode upon him in the gate, and he died, as the man of God had said, who spake when the king came down to him.
II Kings 7:17

And so it fell out unto him: for the people trode upon him in the gate, and he died.
II Kings 7:20

That John the Baptist utilized the gift of the word of knowledge in his ministry is made apparent by the following, from the pen of Luke:

And as the people were in expectation, and all men mused in their hearts of John, whether he were the Christ, or not;

John answered, saying unto them all, I indeed baptize you with water; but one mightier than I cometh, the latchet of whose shoes I am not worthy to unloose: he shall baptize you with the Holy Ghost and with fire:
Luke 3:15-16

John literally answers the unspoken question in a thousand hearts as they confronted him by the river Jordan where he is baptizing. This could be done only by the operation of the gift of the word knowledge.

Jesus ministered as a man ministers. This being so, in order to accomplish the mighty works which characterized His ministry, He of necessity depended on the use of the gifts of the Spirit. One of the outstanding miracles of His ministry was the raising of His young friend to life. We deal with this case further on when studying another of the gifts of the Spirit. For the present I would simply like to show you Jesus exercising the gift of the word of knowledge in connection with the performing of this miracle and some of the incidents surrounding it.

When Lazarus was sick, we read that his sisters sent a **fax or E-mail to Jesus**:

Now a certain man was sick, named Lazarus, of Bethany, the town of Mary and her sister Martha.
John 11:1

Therefore his sisters sent unto him, saying, Lord, behold, he whom thou lovest is sick.

When Jesus heard that, he said, This sickness is not unto death, but for the glory of God, that the Son of God might be glorified thereby.

John 11:3-4

Jesus did not go to Bethany to minister to His friend Lazarus, but He abode yet two days more in the place where He was. But when He knew Lazarus was dead — and no man told Him — He proceeded to make His was to Bethany, and declared boldly to His disciples that Lazarus was dead.

Then said Jesus unto them plainly, Lazarus is dead.
John 11:14

There is but one way whereby He could have known this; that is by the operation of the gift of word of knowledge, that God-given ability to take unto oneself at will a revelation of facts concerning something, concerning anything; a revelation of facts that would be impossible for one to have prior knowledge of.

Then there was the case of the Samaritan woman whom Jesus met at the well of Jacob nigh unto her city.

Then cometh he to a city of Samaria, which is called Sychar, near to the parcel of ground that Jacob gave to his son Joseph.

Now Jacob's well was there. Jesus therefore, being wearied with his journey, sat thus on the well: and it was about the sixth hour.

There cometh a woman of Samaria to draw water: Jesus saith unto her, Give me to drink.

(For his disciples were gone away unto the city to buy meat.)

Then saith the woman of Samaria unto him, How is it that thou, being a Jew, askest drink of me, which am a woman of Samaria? For the Jews have no dealings with the Samaritans.

Jesus answered and said unto her, If thou knewest the gift of God, and who it is that saith to thee, Give me to drink; thou wouldest have asked of him, and he would have given thee living water.

The woman saith unto him, Sir, thou hast nothing to draw with, and the well is deep: from whence then hast thou that living water?

Art thou greater than our father Jacob, which gave us the well, and drank thereof himself, and his children, and his cattle?

Jesus answered and said unto her, Whosoever drinketh of this water shall thirst again:

But whosoever drinketh of the water that I shall give him shall never thirst; but the water that I shall give him shall be in him a well of water springing up into everlasting life.

The woman saith unto him, Sir, give me this water, that I thirst not, neither come hither to draw.

Jesus saith unto her, Go, call thy husband, and come hither.

The woman answered and said, I have no husband. Jesus said unto her, Thou hast well said, I have no husband:

For thou hast had five husbands; and he whom thou now hast is not thy husband: in that saidst thou truly.
John 4:5-18

How could He know about her many husbands, and the fact that she was now living with a man who was not her husband? Only one way: via the operation of the gift of the word of knowledge .

How was Christ able to foretell the fact that Peter would deny Him three times before daybreak (this on the night of His infamous trial in Jerusalem)?

Jesus answered him, Wilt thou lay down thy life for my sake? Verily, verily, I say unto thee, The cock shall not crow, till thou hast denied me thrice.
John 13:38

How could He know that the time had come for Him to be glorified?

And Jesus answered them, saying, The hour is come, that the Son of man should be glorified.
John 12:23

Jesus knew the thoughts of the Pharisees regarding His casting out of devils.

But when the Pharisees heard it, they said, This fellow doth not cast out devils, but by Beelzebub the prince of the devils.

And Jesus knew their thoughts, and said unto them, Every kingdom divided against itself is brought to desolation; and every city or house divided against itself shall not stand:
Matthew 12:24-25

He knew all men and what was in man.

But Jesus did not commit himself unto them, because he knew all men, 25 And needed not that any should testify of man: for he knew what was in man.
John 2:24-25

When He discovered the impotent man at the pool of Bethesda, immediately knew he had been in that condition for a long time.

When Jesus saw him lie, and knew that he had been now a long time in that case, he saith unto him, Wilt thou be made whole?
John 5:6

He knew when His disciples murmured and what they were murmuring about.

When Jesus knew in himself that his disciples murmured at it, he said unto them, Doth this offend you?
John 6:61

One day Jesus said unto His disciples:

a little while, and ye shall not see me: and again, a little while, and ye shall see me, because I go to the Father.
John 16:16

He knew afterwards that they were desirous of asking Him the meaning of this statement.

Now Jesus knew that they were desirous to ask him, and said unto them, Do ye enquire among yourselves of that I said, a little while, and ye shall not see me: and again, a little while, and ye shall see me?
John 16:19

He knew the thoughts of men regarding Himself and the man with the withered hand.

And the scribes and Pharisees watched him, whether he would heal on the sabbath day; that they might find an accusation against him.

But he knew their thoughts, and said to the man which had the withered hand, Rise up, and stand forth in the midst. And he arose and stood forth.
Luke 6:7-8

He perceived the thoughts of those Pharisees and the Scribes who were present when He was ministering to the man who was let down into His presence through the roof, and He answered them.

And the scribes and the Pharisees began to reason, saying, Who is this which speaketh blasphemies? Who can forgive sins, but God alone?

But when Jesus perceived their thoughts, he answering said unto them, What reason ye in your hearts?

Luke 5:21-22

I know of no way of perceiving thoughts other than by the deliberate operation of the gift of the word of knowledge.

He knew all the details regarding the woman Satan had bound.

And ought not this woman, being a daughter of Abraham, whom Satan hath bound, lo, these eighteen years, be loosed from this bond on the sabbath day?
Luke 13:16

(Note: By the operation of the gift of the word of knowledge, Jesus knew that she was a daughter of Abraham, and that she had been bound for eighteen years. As to how He knew it was Satan who had bound her, and what he had bound her with, that required the operation of a different gift, and is dealt with under a separate heading.)

We read of the Apostle Paul coming up to Jerusalem by revelation.

Then fourteen years after I went up again to Jerusalem with Barnabas, and took Titus with me also.

And I went up by revelation, and communicated unto them that gospel which I preach among the Gentiles, but privately to them which were of reputation, lest by any means I should run, or had run, in vain.

Galatians 2:1-2

This simply means that he received, by revelation, the knowledge of the fact that he must go to the city.

Paul received his understanding of the mystery of the Church by the operation of this God-given ability.

How that by revelation he made known unto me the mystery; (as I wrote afore in few words,

Whereby, when ye read, ye may understand my knowledge in the mystery of Christ)

Ephesians 3:3-4

Incidentally, it is Paul who wrote (inferring that this ability to receive knowledge by revelation was not something reserved unto him):

... mention of you in my prayers;

That the God of our Lord Jesus Christ, the Father of glory, may give unto you the spirit of wisdom and revelation in the knowledge of him:

Ephesians 1:16-17

Paul would have been foolish indeed to pray that other believers would receive knowledge by revelation if thought for one moment that this ability was reserved unto himself. The prophet Amos has a word to say about this also.

Surely the Lord GOD will do nothing, but he revealeth his secret unto his servants the prophets.

Amos 3:7

The apostle Peter walked in the use of the gift of the word of knowledge. How else could he have known the facts concerning Ananias and Sapphira? How else could he have known they had agreed together to sell their piece of land, make a presentation of part of the price, and pretend that that part was the whole amount they had received? How else could he have foreknown the fact that they would die for their lying to the Spirit of God, and the further facts concerning the manner in which they would do so?

But a certain man named Ananias, with Sapphira his wife, sold a possession,

And kept back part of the price, his wife also being privy to it, and brought a certain part, and laid it at the apostles' feet.

But Peter said, Ananias, why hath Satan filled thine heart to lie to the Holy Ghost, and to keep back part of the price of the land?

Whiles it remained, was it not thine own? And after it was sold, was it not in thine own power? Why hast thou conceived this thing in thine heart? Thou hast not lied unto men, but unto God.

And Ananias hearing these words fell down, and gave up the ghost: and great fear came on all them that heard these things.

And the young men arose, wound him up, and carried him out, and buried him.

And it was about the space of three hours after, when his wife, not knowing what was done, came in.

And Peter answered unto her, Tell me whether ye sold the land for so much? And she said, Yea, for so much.

Then Peter said unto her, How is it that ye have agreed together to tempt the Spirit of the Lord? Behold, the feet of them which have buried thy husband are at the door, and shall carry thee out.

Then fell she down straightway at his feet, and yielded up the ghost: and the young men came in, and found her dead, and, carrying her forth, buried her by her husband.

Acts 5:1-10

Then there was Nathan, a prophet of God, who, by the operation of the gift of the word of knowledge knew all the details in connection with the little affair between David and Bathsheba, the consequences, etc.

And the LORD sent Nathan unto David. And he came unto him, and said unto him, There were two men in one city; the one rich, and the other poor.

The rich man had exceeding many flocks and herds:

But the poor man had nothing, save one little ewe lamb, which he had bought and nourished up: and it grew up together with him, and with his children; it did eat of his own meat, and drank of his own cup, and lay in his bosom, and was unto him as a daughter.

And there came a traveller unto the rich man, and he spared to take of his own flock and of his own herd, to dress for the wayfaring man that was come unto

69

him; but took the poor man's lamb, and dressed it for the man that was come to him.

And David's anger was greatly kindled against the man; and he said to Nathan, As the LORD liveth, the man that hath done this thing shall surely die:

And he shall restore the lamb fourfold, because he did this thing, and because he had no pity.

II Samuel 12:1-6

And Nathan said to David, Thou art the man. Thus saith the LORD God of Israel, I anointed thee king over Israel, and I delivered thee out of the hand of Saul;

And I gave thee thy master's house, and thy master's wives into thy bosom, and gave thee the house of Israel and of Judah; and if that had been too little, I would moreover have given unto thee such and such things.

Wherefore hast thou despised the commandment of the LORD, to do evil in his sight? Thou hast killed Uriah the Hittite with the sword, and hast taken his wife to be thy wife, and hast slain him with the sword of the children of Ammon.

Now therefore the sword shall never depart from thine house; because thou hast despised me, and hast taken the wife of Uriah the Hittite to be thy wife.

Thus saith the LORD, Behold, I will raise up evil against thee out of thine own house, and I will take thy wives before thine eyes, and give them unto thy neighbour, and he shall lie with thy wives in the sight of this sun.

For thou didst it secretly: but I will do this thing before all Israel, and before the sun.

And David said unto Nathan, I have sinned against the LORD. And Nathan said unto David, The LORD also hath put away thy sin; thou shalt not die.

Howbeit, because by this deed thou hast given great occasion to the enemies of the LORD to blaspheme, the child also that is born unto thee shall surely die.

II Samuel 12:7-14

Without a doubt, Nathan knew the things he was declaring, by the operation of the gift of the word of knowledge. Incidentally, the judgments declared came to pass.

Sometimes the revelation has to do with a moral, or sometimes spiritual problem in the lives of those to whom one ministers. Please remember that the operation of all spiritual gifts is to be unto the building up of the Church.

How is it then, brethren? When ye come together, every one of you hath a psalm, hath a doctrine, hath a tongue, hath a revelation, hath an interpretation. Let all things be done unto edifying.
I Corinthians 14:26

The product of the operation of the gifts (which constitutes the manifestation of the Spirit) is to be unto benefit.

But the manifestation of the Spirit is given to every man to profit withal.
I Corinthians 12:7

Positive proof that the previous reference is associated with the operation of the gifts of the Spirit is the fact that immediately following this verse, and connected therewith, God has listed those things which we bring into existence when we utilize these supernatural abilities. With reference to the operation of the gift of the word of knowledge, this is specially so; that is, it is specially important that the manifestation be unto benefit.

Revelations concerning moral and spiritual problems in the lives of our brothers and sisters are not given to us that we may exploit, but rather that we may restore, those who have fallen by the wayside.

Brethren, if a man be overtaken in a fault, ye which are spiritual, restore such an one in the spirit of meekness; considering thyself, lest thou also be tempted.
Galatians 6:1

Because of the very natural of this gift and of its operation, love is required in the hearts of those to whom it is entrusted .

And though I have the gift of prophecy, and understand all mysteries, and all knowledge; and though I have all faith, so that I could remove mountains, and have not charity, I am nothing.
I Corinthians 13:2

It is for the same reason that the Lord has so closely linked together the gift of the word of knowledge and the gift of the word of wisdom, which we will study next. Throughout the Scriptures, you will notice that those who possessed the one usually possessed the other.

Wise men lay up knowledge: but the mouth of the foolish is near destruction.
Proverbs 10:14

The fear of the LORD is the beginning of wisdom: and the knowledge of the holy is understanding.

Proverbs 9:10

Cease, my son, to hear the instruction that causeth to err from the words of knowledge.

Proverbs 19:27

CHAPTER FIVE

THE GIFT OF THE WORD OF WISDOM

And Joshua the son of Nun was full of the spirit of wisdom; for Moses had laid his hands upon him: and the children of Israel hearkened unto him, and did as the LORD commanded Moses.
Deuteronomy 34:9

As the gift of tongues is circumscribed in its sphere of operation except the gift of the interpretation of tongues be in operation in conjunction with it, so also the gift of word of knowledge is exercised under handicap without the possession and use of the gift of the word of wisdom.

WHAT IT IS NOT

The gift of the word of wisdom is not human wisdom increased, sanctified, or blessed of God. It has nothing to do with becoming wise, discreet, shrewd in understanding and judgement. The simple-minded can possess and exercise well the gift of the word of wisdom.

WHAT IT IS

The gift of the word of wisdom is the God-given ability to take unto yourself, at will, at your will, a revelation of what to do about a situation once you do know the facts concerning the case. The revelation thus received is known as a word of wisdom.

We see this gift in operation in the life and ministry of Joseph. With reference to his interpretation of the dream of the Pharaoh of Egypt relative to the coming famine (which interpretation was the fruit of his deliberate exercise of the gift of the word of knowledge) we read that he gave the king counsel and advice as to what to do about the situation to the end that life might be reserved.

Now therefore let Pharaoh look out a man discreet and wise, and set him over the land of Egypt.

Let Pharaoh do this, and let him appoint officers over the land, and take up the fifth part of the land of Egypt in the seven plenteous years.

And let them gather all the food of those good years that come, and lay up corn under the hand of Pharaoh, and let them keep food in the cities.

And that food shall be for store to the land against the seven years of famine, which shall be in the land of Egypt; that the land perish not through the famine.
Genesis 41:33-36

Joseph was a foreigner, a stranger in Egypt, sold into slavery by his own brethren when he was but a lad. His education was far from complete. Add to this his years of imprisonment in an Egyptian dungeon without contact with the outside world, and you can readily see that the advice he gave the king was not based on the wisdom of man.

Being a stranger, and uneducated, he would know nothing of the statistics of the country. Its annual grain production and consumption, the amount usually shipped to other lands, would be unknown quantities to him. He would have no knowledge of the birth rate, death rate, record of marriages, immigration, and emigration. In short, in the natural realm he had nothing upon which to base his decision as to what to do about this drastic situation. Yet his advice was so terrific that the Pharaoh, quick to realize the immensity of it, at once appointed him Prime Minister of Egypt.

With the next fourteen years of Egypt's history naked before his eyes (half of that period of time years of superabundance, the other half years of very severe famine) natural reasoning would have suggested dividing the annual harvest into two equal parts, saving half for the years of drought.

By the way, what about shrinkage, and loss by fire and theft? What about preserving a bit of seed for the first planting once the good years commenced again? What about grain required for barter? Oh, there are so many angles to this case; so many things to be taken into consideration. But Joseph declared that one fifth part of the total annual production of Egypt was sufficient to keep each year, in store for those years of famine ahead. One fifth was sufficient, not only for her own needs but for the meeting of the needs of those who might come to her from other lands for help during that time.

Here's another thought. Why did Joseph, a man of God, not urge the king to proclaim a fast? Why did he not suggest repentance and a turning to God as the remedy for the situation? Because the thing was established.

And for that the dream was doubled unto Pharaoh twice; it is because the thing is established by God, and God will shortly bring it to pass.
Genesis 41:32

God's Word decrees

...that in the mouth of two or three witnesses every word may be established.
Matt. 18:16B

It was too late to prevent the proclamation from coming to pass.

It is certain, no matter how you approach the subject, that the counsel and advice he gave the king was the product of his deliberate operation of the gift of the word wisdom.

Via the operation of this gift, Daniel showed king Nebuchadnezzar what to do to avoid the sure judgement which was coming his way. (Incidentally, the judgement and the fact that it was coming had been revealed by the operation of the gift of the word of knowledge.)

Wherefore, O king, let my counsel be acceptable unto thee, and break off thy sins by righteousness, and thine iniquities by shewing mercy to the poor; if it may be a lengthening of thy tranquillity.
Daniel 4:27

As Moses led his people into the wilderness toward Canaan, his father-law, Jethro, high priest of Midian, came to visit.

And it came to pass on the morrow, that Moses sat to judge the people: and the people stood by Moses from the morning unto the evening.

And when Moses' father in law saw all that he did to the people, he said, What is this thing that thou doest to the people? Why sittest thou thyself alone, and all the people stand by thee from morning unto even?

And Moses said unto his father in law, Because the people come unto me to enquire of God:

When they have a matter, they come unto me; and I judge between one and another, and I do make them know the statutes of God, and his laws.
Exodus 18:13-16

At this time Jethro gave his son-in-law counsel and advice to the end that he and the nation might survive and make progress in their march toward the land God had promised them.

And Moses' father in law said unto him, The thing that thou doest is not good.

Thou wilt surely wear away, both thou, and this people that is with thee: for this thing is too heavy for thee; thou art not able to perform it thyself alone.

Hearken now unto my voice, I will give thee counsel, and God shall be with thee: Be thou for the people to God-ward, that thou mayest bring the causes unto God:

And thou shalt teach them ordinances and laws, and shalt shew them the way wherein they must walk, and the work that they must do.

Moreover thou shalt provide out of all the people able men, such as fear God, men of truth, hating covetousness; and place such over them, to be rulers of thousands, and rulers of hundreds, rulers of fifties, and rulers of tens:

And let them judge the people at all seasons: and it shall be, that every great matter they shall bring unto thee, but every small matter they shall judge: so shall it be easier for thyself, and they shall bear the burden with thee.

If thou shalt do this thing, and God command thee so, then thou shalt be able to endure, and all this people shall also go to their place in peace.

Exodus 18:17-23

Even a casual survey of the above Scriptures will suffice to convince any open heart that Jethro's counsel was the product of the operation of the gift of the word of wisdom.

Joshua had this gift.

And Joshua the son of Nun was full of the spirit of wisdom; for Moses had laid his hands upon him: and the children of Israel hearkened unto him, and did as the LORD commanded Moses.

Deuteronomy 34:9

This verse also states that he received this gift by the laying on of hands of Moses. It all happened when God spoke to Moses concerning his death and the appointing of a successor.

And the LORD said unto Moses, Take thee Joshua the son of Nun, a man in whom is the spirit, and lay thine hand upon him;

And set him before Eleazar the priest, and before all the congregation; and give him a charge in their sight.

And thou shalt put some of thine honour upon him, that all the congregation of the children of Israel may be obedient.

And he shall stand before Eleazar the priest, who shall ask counsel for him after the judgment of Urim before the LORD: at his word shall they go out, and at his word they shall come in, both he, and all the children of Israel with him, even all the congregation.

And Moses did as the LORD commanded him: and he took Joshua, and set him before Eleazar the priest, and before all the congregation:

And he laid his hands upon him, and gave him a charge, as the LORD commanded by the hand of Moses.

Numbers 27:18-23

Note: "The Spirit of wisdom" is Old Testament phraseology for the gift of the word of wisdom.

Solomon prayed for the gift of the word of wisdom and the gift of the word of knowledge.

In that night did God appear unto Solomon, and said unto him, Ask what I shall give thee.

And Solomon said unto God, Thou hast shewed great mercy unto David my father, and hast made me to reign in his stead.

Now, O LORD God, let thy promise unto David my father be established: for thou hast made me king over a people like the dust of the earth in multitude.

Give me now wisdom and knowledge, that I may go out and come in before this people: for who can judge this thy people, that is so great?
II Chronicles 1:7-10

God was pleased with the request of Solomon so much so that He not only granted it, He added to the young king much more.

And God said to Solomon, Because this was in thine heart, and thou hast not asked riches, wealth, or honour, nor the life of thine enemies, neither yet hast asked long life; but hast asked wisdom and knowledge for thyself, that thou mayest judge my people, over whom I have made thee king:

Wisdom and knowledge is granted unto thee; and I will give thee riches, and wealth, and honour, such as none of the kings have had that have been before thee, neither shall there any after thee have the like.
II Chronicles 1:11-12

So Solomon, the son of David, took the throne, and we see him, for the first time, holding court.

Then came there two women, that were harlots, unto the king, and stood before him.

And the one woman said, O my lord, I and this woman dwell in one house; and I was delivered of a child with her in the house.

And it came to pass the third day after that I was delivered, that this woman was delivered also: and we were together; there was no stranger with us in the house, save we two in the house.

And this woman's child died in the night; because she overlaid it.

And she arose at midnight, and took my son from beside me, while thine handmaid slept, and laid it in her bosom, and laid her dead child in my bosom.

And when I rose in the morning to give my child suck, behold, it was dead: but when I had considered it in the morning, behold, it was not my son, which I did bear.

And the other woman said, Nay; but the living is my son, and the dead is thy son. And this said, No; but the dead is thy son, and the living is my son. Thus they spake before the king.
I Kings 3:16-22

Solomon is confronted with a real problem. Two Hebrew women who are harlots stand before him. They have between them one living child, each one claiming to be the mother thereof. It is his first public act since ascending the throne. The eyes of his courties are upon him. Will he judge righteous judgement?

Then said the king, The one saith, This is my son that liveth, and thy son is the dead: and the other saith, Nay; but thy son is the dead, and my son is the living.

And the king said, Bring me a sword. And they brought a sword before the king.   **I Kings 3:23-24**

A shock swept the courtroom, jarring everyone's soul therein. David's reign was a rough one. He was known as a man of blood. In fact, many times David acted as executioner as well as judge. His once-familiar cry, "off with his head, off with his head" had not been heard for some time, for David is dead.

The people were sick of blood. Yes, David did consolidate the kingdom and they were grateful, but to accomplish this he, of necessity, ruled with a rod of iron. However, David's work was accomplished. He had gone on. Surely the sword of the executioner may rest! Will his son follow in his father's footsteps?

It was a time of trouble, or near trouble. Adonijah, half brother to the king, had attempted to usurp the throne. It has proved to be a abortive attempt; still its imprint is felt upon then nation. Some are staunch supporters of the usurper. Others wonder in their hearts. The tension in the nation was high. Anything could happen.

"Bring me a sword."

Involuntarily men feel for their throats. Eyes meet across the court. The universal thought is "here we go again."

And the king said, Bring me a sword. And they brought a sword before the king.
I Kings 3:24

Action! A new tension sweeps the people. What will he do?   The two women stand speechless, helpless in the hands of powerful eunuchs who hold them lest they tear each other apart with their bare hands. They are mothers, Hebrew mothers, fighting over a child. You have a real situation here. Their words have been hasty, the argument bitter, as they presented their case before the king.

And the other woman said, Nay; but the living is my son, and the dead is thy son. And this said, No; but the dead is thy son, and the living is my son. Thus they spake before the king.
I Kings 3:22

There is fire in their words. Eyes flashing, spitting on the floor in typical Hebrew fashion, they pronounce judgement and anathema the one upon the other; bloodshed is prevented only because they are held helpless in the hands of the king's servants.

The executioner waits, sword in hand. He has been idle since king David passed away. The tension increases. Has the king decided which is the guilty party? Will he slay one or both? a courtier, ruler of a province, whispers in the ear of his fellow, 'just like his father." another murmurs, "And I thought we might be through with blood, he being such a young man, and kind looking.

And the king said, Divide the living child in two, and give half to the one, and half to the other.
I Kings 3:25

Oh, no! He can't be serious! This can't be! Men sicken within. "Divide the living child in two." He speaks as though he were talking about a pound of butter or a fish! Divide the living child in two! Is the man crazy? Women gasp. At least one is fainting. "Divide the living child in two." The executioner steps forward, raises his sword, reaches for the baby.

A woman's scream rends the air. A woman has gone wild. She tears herself free from the hands of her captors; she throws herself between the sword and her baby. No! No! Don't you dare. Give her the little one. Let her have my baby; but don't you dare touch him." She turns to the king and cries:

Then spake the woman whose the living child was unto the king, for her bowels yearned upon her son, and she said, O my lord, give her the living child, and in no wise slay it. But the other said, Let it be neither mine nor thine, but divide it.   **I Kings 3:26**

The other woman is undisturbed. Calmly adjusting an earring, she then speaks.

> **Then spake the woman whose the living child was unto the king, for her bowels yearned upon her son, and she said, O my lord, give her the living child, and in no wise slay it. But the other said, Let it be neither mine nor thine, but divide it.**
>
> **I Kings 3:26**

She has no mother's heart of love for this little one. Her inward parts are not bleeding for his safety. She is not concerned for his life. "Divide the child." She is saving her face.

But the mother of the living child stands between the blade and her darling, every fibre of her being alive with love, passion, purpose and determination, ready to die for the life of her baby. There is but one way to reach the child to its hurt; over her dead body. They will have to carve their way through this mother to reach her child. And not only the king, but all present, can see who is the mother of the living child.

> **Then the king answered and said, Give her the living child, and in no wise slay it: she is the mother thereof.**
>
> **I Kings 3:27**

The tension is gone. The people breathe freely again. Tongues begin to wag. Courtiers are busy conversing excitedly with each other. The news spreads. People rejoice. Adonijah no longer poses a problem. He is no longer a threat to the peace of the land. This one shall be king; a king worthy of honor; a king worthy of peace. Peace upon his head. Long live King Solomon! And the kingdom is established in the hands of Solomon, son of David.

> **And all Israel heard of the judgment which the king had judged; and they feared the king: for they saw that the wisdom of God was in him, to do judgment.**
>
> **I Kings 3:28**

Yes, Solomon possessed this marvellous God-given ability, the gift of the word of wisdom as it is referred to in the New Testament phraseology, and he used it to the establishing of his kingdom, ruling God's people and ruling them well.

I now wish to show you the gift of the word of wisdom being utilized in conjunction with the word of knowledge in the ministry of Jesus Christ Himself.

Lazarus, a personal friend of Jesus of Nazareth, was dead, and Jesus came from beyond Jordan unto Bethany to Mary and Martha, sisters of the deceased. The fact that Mary and Martha were sisters and that Lazarus was their brother, the Scriptures affirm.

Now a certain man was sick, named Lazarus, of Bethany, the town of Mary and her sister Martha.

(It was that Mary which anointed the Lord with ointment, and wiped his feet with her hair, whose brother Lazarus was sick.)

Therefore his sisters sent unto him, saying, Lord, behold, he whom thou lovest is sick.

John 11:1-3

When Jesus knew that Lazarus was dead, (and this He knew by the operation of the gift of the word knowledge) He went to Bethany. Here He met Martha.

Then Martha, as soon as she heard that Jesus was coming, went and met him: but Mary sat still in the house.

Then said Martha unto Jesus, Lord, if thou hadst been here, my brother had not died.

But I know, that even now, whatsoever thou wilt ask of God, God will give it thee.

Jesus saith unto her, Thy brother shall rise again.

Martha saith unto him, I know that he shall rise again in the resurrection at the last day.

Jesus said unto her, I am the resurrection, and the life: he that believeth in me, though he were dead, yet shall he live:

And whosoever liveth and believeth in me shall never die. Believest thou this?

She saith unto him, Yea, Lord: I believe that thou art the Christ, the Son of God, which should come into the world.

John 11:20-27

Later that day, Mary came to meet Jesus.

Then when Mary was come where Jesus was, and saw him, she fell down at his feet, saying unto him, Lord, if thou hadst been here, my brother had not died.

When Jesus therefore saw her weeping, and the Jews also weeping which came with her, he groaned in the spirit, and was troubled,

And said, Where have ye laid him? They said unto him, Lord, come and see.

Jesus wept.

John 11:32-35

At first glance it seems a strange, both sisters utilizing the same expression upon meeting Christ. They have but one thought in mind: if Jesus had been here, if He had arrived in time their brother would not be in that tomb.

Then said Martha unto Jesus, Lord, if thou hadst been here, my brother had not died.

John 11:21

Then when Mary was come where Jesus was, and saw him, she fell down at his feet, saying unto him, Lord, if thou hadst been here, my brother had not died.

John 11:32

Christ's response, however, differed in each case. In fact, there is an eternity of difference between His two response! He responded to Martha by skillfully guiding her to acknowledgment of Himself as a personal Saviour. When Mary approached Him with the identical statement, He wept. The truth of the matter is that Mary was already converted. She was the harlot who knelt at His feet in the house of Simon the Pharisee.

And one of the Pharisees desired him that he would eat with him. And he went into the Pharisee's house, and sat down to meat.

And, behold, a woman in the city, which was a sinner, when she knew that Jesus sat at meat in the Pharisee's house, brought an alabaster box of ointment,

And stood at his feet behind him weeping, and began to wash his feet with tears, and did wipe them with the hairs of her head, and kissed his feet, and anointed them with the ointment.

Luke 7:36-38

That Mary, sister of Martha, was this same harlot is proven by the following text:

(It was that Mary which anointed the Lord with ointment, and wiped his feet with her hair, whose brother Lazarus was sick.)

John 11:2

One day Jesus sat in the house of His friends at Bethany. Mary was conversing with Him of things pertaining to His Kingdom, while Martha was preparing dinner. Apparently Jesus had previously dealt with her concerning spiritual things. She entered the room, and Jesus, utilizing spiritual abilities, perceived her turmoil of soul and said unto her:

And Jesus answered and said unto her, Martha, Martha, thou art careful and troubled about many things:
Luke 10:41

To this day many people unwittingly accuse Jesus of being ungracious, unkind, unappreciative. They say He rebuked Martha because she was fussing around getting dinner ready for Him. His words do not constitute a rebuke. He merely capitalized on the opportunity to bring before her mind a thought from which she would never be able to free herself until she was converted.

She was troubled about many things, He said. She was a good woman. Her sister, on the other hand, had been a harlot. Could this be one of the many things? She saw the change in Mary since Christ had come into her life. Perhaps this troubled her as well. Of one thing we are certain: Jesus, perceiving her turmoil of soul, drew her attention to it, and to the fact that it was not hidden from His eyes.

The fact that Mary was already converted is proven. Continuing to address Martha, Jesus said:

But one thing is needful: and Mary hath chosen that good part, which shall not be taken away from her.
Luke 10:42

She was speaking of the eternal life which she, Mary now possessed in Him:

And I give unto them eternal life; and they shall never perish, neither shall any man pluck them out of my hand.
John 10:28

Mary was converted in the house of Simon the Pharisee.

And he said to the woman, Thy faith hath saved thee; go in peace.
Luke 7:50

The foregoing makes apparent the reason for the difference in the responses. Christ saw this moment of crisis in her life as the moment He had been waiting for. She was troubled. Her mind was filled with misinterpretations of the Scriptures. He set her thinking straight. He exposed her perplexities. She saw the light and was converted.

When Mary approached Him, He simply suffered with her in His great heart of love. She had already become a partaker of the divine nature. She was already born again.

When He met Martha near the tomb of her brother, He finished the work He had commenced earlier, and won her to Himself. This was the fulfillment of His own prophecy;

> **When Jesus heard that, he said, This sickness is not unto death, but for the glory of God, that the Son of God might be glorified thereby.**
> **John 11:4**

When He met Mary near that same tomb there was no work of grace to perform. It had already been accomplished.

The Pharisees and Herodians approached Jesus with a question concerning the tribute money, in an effect to entangle Him in His speech so that they might have somewhat of which to accuse Him.

> **Then went the Pharisees, and took counsel how they might entangle him in his talk.**
>
> **And they sent out unto him their disciples with the Herodians, saying, Master, we know that thou art true, and teachest the way of God in truth, neither carest thou for any man: for thou regardest not the person of men.**
>
> **Tell us therefore, What thinkest thou? Is it lawful to give tribute unto Caesar, or not?**
>
> **But Jesus perceived their wickedness, and said, Why tempt ye me, ye hypocrites?**
>
> **Shew me the tribute money. And they brought unto him a penny.**
>
> **And he saith unto them, Whose is this image and superscription?**
>
> **They say unto him, Caesar's. Then saith he unto them, Render therefore unto Caesar the things which are Caesar's; and unto God the things that are God's.**
> **Matthew 22:15-21**

Jesus was in a predicament. Uphold the paying of the tribute to Rome, and His ministry would be a thing of the past. The people would turn against Him. They would have grounds for laying charges against Him before the religious court of Israel. Take His stand against the paying of the tribute, and they would accuse Him unto the Roman authorities.

The prosecution could easily be pressed on charges of teaching insurrection, rebellion, and treason against the state. The very soldiers, a Roman soldier on guard duty in the temple, would have arrested Him on the spot. By the operation of both the gift of the word of knowledge and the gift of the word of wisdom, Jesus foiled the plot of His enemies, saving Himself in a very delicate situation.

Paul and Barnabas conducted a revival at Antioch of the Gentiles. Multitudes believed the gospel of the grace of God and were converted.

And certain men which came down from Judaea taught the brethren, and said, Except ye be circumcised after the manner of Moses, ye cannot be saved.

When therefore Paul and Barnabas had no small dissension and disputation with them, they determined that Paul and Barnabas, and certain other of them, should go up to Jerusalem unto the apostles and elders about this question.

And being brought on their way by the church, they passed through Phenice and Samaria, declaring the conversion of the Gentiles: and they caused great joy unto all the brethren.

And when they were come to Jerusalem, they were received of the church, and of the apostles and elders, and they declared all things that God had done with them.

But there rose up certain of the sect of the Pharisees which believed, saying, That it was needful to circumcise them, and to command them to keep the law of Moses.

And the apostles and elders came together for to consider of this matter.
Acts 15:1-6

The theology of these self-appointed teachers was simple: "We are Jews. We were duly circumcised. We kept the law of Moses. Now we have accepted Jesus Christ as our Saviour, and we are saved. You have accepted Him. Now keep the law of Moses; be circumcised and you will be saved. We will both have done all. Nothing will have been left undone.

Our doughty disciples of Christ withstood these teachers to the face, of cause. Finally the church paid their way to Jerusalem, there to take up this matter with the elders. En route they preached in the various churches, declaring the conversion of the Gentiles and causing much joy thereby.

At Jerusalem a conference was called. The charges were laid. Peter called to mind the fact that Cornelius' household had received the baptism with the Holy Spirit under his ministry before they were baptized in water, let alone being circumcised, or having kept any of the precepts of Moses. He concluded his discourse with the following:

But we believe that through the grace of the Lord Jesus Christ we shall be saved, even as they.
Acts 15:11

Natural wisdom would never have couched this statement in those words; rather the reverse. They, even as we, would have been the order if the wisdom of man was dictating. This marvelously-presented bit of argument was followed by the testimonies of Paul and Barnabas as they declared the signs and wonders wrought under their hands in the Antioch revival, with all present rejoicing at the news.

Then James took the stand, and, confirming by the Scriptures the visitation of God among the Gentiles, he made a suggestion that letters be written encouraging these new Christians to live for God and to abstain from four things (things any sane person should desire to abstain from).

The opposition quickly embraced this opportunity to do their little bit. In writing they referred to Barnabas and Paul in a manner which would warm the hearts of the Gentiles.

It seemed good unto us, being assembled with one accord, to send chosen men unto you with our beloved Barnabas and Paul,

Men that have hazarded their lives for the name of our Lord Jesus Christ.
Acts 15:25-26

When the Gentile believers heard these words, their hearts waxed warm toward the elders at Jerusalem; they felt better about the teachers who had started all this trouble; they accepted the admonitions contained in the epistle, and the revival continued. The teachers from amongst the believing Pharisees were happy because they had been allowed to write at least some manner of instruction in righteousness to these Christians, and because it had been so graciously received. The elders were content. Paul and Barnabas rejoiced in the victory. Everybody was happy, and a split in the church had been avoided. Anyone with an unbiased mind can readily see the gift of the word of wisdom being utilized here. **Compare that with the average church conference today!**

James draws our attention to a man who possessed both the gift of the word of knowledge and the gift of the word of wisdom.

Who is a wise man and endued with knowledge among you? Let him shew out of a good conversation his works with meekness of wisdom.
James 3:13

The product of the operation of the gift of the word of wisdom is known by its attributes.

1.   **It is pure.**
2.   **It is peaceable.**
3.   **It is gentle.**
4.   **It is easy to be entreated.**

Just as definitely as the foregoing are enumerated, we find two elements of which the product of the operation of the gift of the word of wisdom is full.

1.   **It full of mercy.**
2.   **It is full of good fruits.**

Just as surely, we find listed in the same verse two elements of which there is no trace in a word of wisdom.

1.   **It is without partially.**
2.   **It is without hypocrisy.**

Think it over and you will see very readily that the gift of the word of wisdom is very necessary and would be a God-send if in use amongst God's people today.

And that he would shew thee the secrets of wisdom...
Job 11:6

CHAPTER SIX

THE GIFT OF THE DISCERNING OF SPIRITS

And they shall teach my people the difference between the holy and profane, and cause them to discern between the unclean and the clean.
Ezekiel 44:23

WHAT IT IS NOT:

It is not the gift of discerment; there is no such gift. Discernment is astuteness in judgment, insight, a purely natural ability. It is not the gift of criticism, neither is it the gift of suspicion.

WHAT IT IS:

It is the God-given ability to detect the presence and ascertain the identity of spirits, and spirits only. There is such a thing as the gift of discerning of men.

One should not confuse the discerning of spirits with the casting out of devils. The casting out of devils is an act on the part of the believer ministering. The gift of the discerning of spirits is the God-given ability to perform a certain act, but the act is the discerning, not the casting out of spirits.

Now to disuss this gift properly, an understanding (at lease in part) of spirits is required. The subject is a vast one.

ALL LIFE IS SPIRIT

There is a spirit in man...Job 32:8

In the beginning:

> **And the LORD God formed man of the dust of the ground, and breathed into his nostrils the breath of life; and man became a living soul.**
> **Genesis 2:7**

The breath of life is known as
the spirit of man which is in him....1Cor. 2:11

This life (all spirit is life and all life is spirit) is in the blood.

> **For the life of the flesh is in the blood.**
> **Leviticus 17:11**

It is this life (spirit) in a man which keeps him alive. By the same token, death is the departing of that spirit (life). This is attested to by the Word of God in connection with the raising of the daughter of Jairus from the dead.

And he put them all out, and took her by the hand, and called, saying, Maid, arise.

And her spirit came again, and she arose straightway: and he commanded to give her meat.
Luke 8:54-55

When a person dies, the spirit (life) leaves the body. Having come from God in the first place, it nows returns to Him.

Then shall the dust return to the earth as it was: and the spirit shall return unto God who gave it.

At death, the spirit of man goes up.

Who knoweth the spirit of man that goeth upward, and the spirit of the beast that goeth downward to the earth?
Ecclesiastes 3:21

In the beginning man was made.

And God said, let us make man...Gen. 1:26

To make anything, substance is required.

And the LORD God formed man of the dust of the ground, and breathed into his nostrils the breath of life; and man became a living soul.
Genesis 2:7

The Almighty took dust of the earth, formed it into a shape, and declared that shape was the "form" of man. Therefore that "form" was, and is, the "form" of man. This word is commonly used in the Scriptures to designate man's body, his design, etc. It is also used much in making plain the fact that man is actually God's handiwork.

Adam was first formed, then Eve. ...1Tim. 2:13

David, in one of his most outsiding psalms, declares that God

formed the eye...Psm. 94:9

Ehihu testifies to the same truth.

The Spirit of God hath made me...

Continuing his testimony, he declares

the breath of the Almighty hath given me life.
Job 33:4

He makes a further statement to the effect that God fashioned him, and fashioned him of earth.

I also am formed out of clay Job.33:6

In the book of the prophet Isaiah, God sums up the entire matter conclusively. Speaking of the bringing of man into existence He says:

Even every one that is called by my name: for I have created him for my glory,
I have formed him; yea, I have made him.
Isaiah 43:7

That God made man, formed man, and created man, there can be no vestige of doubt. That these terms are not synonymous is just as apparent. To make, one requires substances. The thing made must, of necessity, be given some sort of shape; it must be formed. When one creates, he produces something out of nothing.

God, therefore did not create man's body. He made it; He formed it; of the dust of the earth He produced it. What He created was in His (God's) image. Man's body is not in the image of God. It is in the form of man.

Nevertherless man, says the Word, was created in the image of God.

So God created man in his own image, in the image of God created he him;
male and female created he them.
Genesis 1:27

God is a Spirit.....John 4:24

Therefore, that part of man which He (God) created is spirit.

The fall of man from his original state demanded a new creation within his being before fellowship with God could be restored. This new creation is the new birth which one experiences through faith in the finished work of Christ., i.e., that which He accomplished for us by the substitutionary death upon the cross.

A Christian therefore, is a person in whom a new spirit exists, i.e., the spirit of Christ.

But ye are not in the flesh, but in the Spirit, if so be that the Spirit of God dwell in you. Now if any man have not the Spirit of Christ, he is none of his.

Romans 8:9

By the same token, if you are one of His, you have His spirit; this is that new spirit which has come into existence and being in your heart.

Therefore if any man be in Christ, he is a new creature: old things are passed away; behold, all things are become new.
2 Corinthians 5:17

This is that new man:

And that ye put on the new man, which after God is created in righteousness and true holiness.
Ephesians 4:24

This new man is created in the image of God:

And have put on the new man, which is renewed in knowledge after the image of him that created him:
Colossians 3:10

Angels are spirits. The Word of God makes this plain.

And of the angels he saith, Who maketh his angels spirits, and his ministers a flame of fire.
Hebrews 1:7

God created them all. But there was war in heaven. Lucifer, brightest of the sons of the morning, second only to God Almighty Himself in power, beauty, and wisdom, rebelled against his Creator, and cajoled one third of the heavenly host into rebellion also.

And there was war in heaven:

And there was war in heaven: Michael and his angels fought against the dragon; and the dragon fought and his angels,

And prevailed not; neither was their place found any more in heaven.

And the great dragon was cast out, that old serpent, called the Devil, and Satan, which deceiveth the whole world: he was cast out into the earth, and his angels were cast out with him.

Revelation 12:7-9

The reason for the rebellion was from Lucifer's desire to usurp God's throne, and to be as God Himself.

For thou hast said in thine heart, I will ascend into heaven, I will exalt my throne above the stars of God: I will sit also upon the mount of the congregation, in the sides of the north:

I will ascend above the heights of the clouds; I will be like the most High.

Isaiah 14:13-14

Satan was Lucifer falling from heaven.

How art thou fallen from heaven, O Lucifer, son of the morning! how art thou cut down to the ground, which didst weaken the nations!

Isaiah 14:12

He, Lucifer, is now known as the Devil, and Satan. The angels that fell with him are known as his, this automatically leaving him in complete control of them all. Hell was prepared specificallly for them.

... everlasting fire, prepared for the devil and his angels:

Matthew 25:41

The spirit world, therefore, spreads itself before us, a great panorama. There is God Himself, Who always was, and Who always will be. He is a spirit. He alone is holy. He is the Holy Spirit.

There are the angels of God: Michael the Archangel; Gabriel, who is known in the Scriptures as the angel of the Lord; and multitudes of other angels, millions of created spirits, all good.

There is the spirit of man in each man. There are those who are born; in each one of these dwells a new spirit, a spirit which is born of God, created in His image.

There are the millions of fallen angels, and Lucifer himself, now known as Satan and the Devil. Besides all this, the Lord God spoke to the serpent (Satan himself) in the garden of Eden and, while declaring judgement upon him for the part he played in procuring the fall of men, mentioned his seed.

93

And I will put enmity between thee and the woman, and between thy seed and her seed; it shall bruise thy head, and thou shalt bruise his heel.
Genesis 3:15

Four thousand years later, Christ faced a group of priests in the temple at Jerusalem.

I know that ye are Abraham's seed; but ye seek to kill me, because my word hath no place in you.

I speak that which I have seen with my Father: and ye do that which ye have seen with your father.

They answered and said unto him, Abraham is our father. Jesus saith unto them, If ye were Abraham's children, ye would do the works of Abraham.

But now ye seek to kill me, a man that hath told you the truth, which I have heard of God: this did not Abraham.

Ye do the deeds of your father. Then said they to him, We be not born of fornication; we have one Father, even God.

Jesus said unto them, If God were your Father, ye would love me: for I proceeded forth and came from God; neither came I of myself, but he sent me.

Why do ye not understand my speech? even because ye cannot hear my word.

Ye are of your father the devil, and the lusts of your father ye will do. He was a murderer from the beginning, and abode not in the truth, because there is no truth in him. When he speaketh a lie, he speaketh of his own: for he is a liar, and the father of it.
John 8:37-44

Jesus acknowledged them as Abraham's seed, yet declared Abraham was not their father, and finally declared them to be their father the devil.

Jesus was not using a figure of speech here. Rather, He was being very specific. He was not adddressing the flesh when He called them the seed of the serpent, but was addressing the evil spirits resident in these men. These evil spirits were not fallen angels, for such cannot be the seed of Satan: they were created by God Almighty. These spirits were begotten of Satan. They were his offspring, his seed.

So our spirit world has grown. And the two great camps therein are opposed the one to the other as diametrically as day and night are opposed the one to the other.

94

In the spirit world, therefore, a great and continuous battle rages. It is between God Almighty with His angels of heaven and Satan with his hosts. Man (natural man) understands it not.

But the natural man receiveth not the things of the Spirit of God: for they are foolishness unto him: neither can he know them, because they are spiritually discerned.
1 Corinthians 2:14

God has not left His people helpless against the onslaughts of the enemy. He has provided spiritual armament and armour for us whom He has called into this battle with Him, and He exhorts us to put it on.

Finally, my brethren, be strong in the Lord, and in the power of his might.

Put on the whole armour of God, that ye may be able to stand against the wiles of the devil.

For we wrestle not against flesh and blood, but against principalities, against powers, against the rulers of the darkness of this world, against spiritual wickedness in high places.

Wherefore take unto you the whole armour of God, that ye may be able to withstand in the evil day, and having done all, to stand.

Stand therefore, having your loins girt about with truth, and having on the breastplate of righteousness;

And your feet shod with the preparation of the gospel of peace;

Above all, taking the shield of faith, wherewith ye shall be able to quench all the fiery darts of the wicked.

And take the helmet of salvation, and the sword of the Spirit, which is the word of God:
Ephesians 6:10-17

God fully understands our inability to cope with supernatural forces in our natural strength and wisdom. Therefore, He has provided supernatural abilities, the gifts of the Spirit, and He says to us concerning them:

Now concerning spiritual gifts, brethren, I would not have you ignorant.
1 Corinthians 12:1

He says unto us:

Behold, I give unto you power to tread on serpents and scorpions, and over all the power of the enemy: and nothing shall by any means hurt you.
Luke 10:19

His Word declares that we shall receive power after we have been baptized with the Holy Ghost.

But ye shall receive power, after that the Holy Ghost is come upon you: and ye shall be witnesses unto me both in Jerusalem, and in all Judaea, and in Samaria, and unto the uttermost part of the earth.
Acts 1:8

Far too many of God's people do not realize that the term "power" as it is used here, signifies ability. It could as well be written: I make you able. It means the same thing; able to cast out devils; able to heal the sick; able ministers of the new covenant. This infers the receiving and utilization of spiritual gifts, i.e., God-given abilities, for by these and your use of them only are you made able; only by your deliberate use of them have you power over the enemy.

God intended us to receive and utilize the gifts of the spirit to the tearing down of the strongholds of Satan.

For though we walk in the flesh, we do not war after the flesh:

(For the weapons of our warfare are not carnal, but mighty through God to the pulling down of strong holds;)

Casting down imaginations, and every high thing that exalteth itself against the knowledge of God, and bringing into captivity every thought to the obedience of Christ;
2 Corinthians 10:3-5

The weapons of our warfare are the gifts of the spirit. These, and all truths connected therewith, are revealed unto us by the Spirit of God.

But as it is written, Eye hath not seen, nor ear heard, neither have entered into the heart of man, the things which God hath prepared for them that love him.

But God hath revealed them unto us by his Spirit: for the Spirit searcheth all things, yea, the deep things of God.
1 Corinthians 2:9-10

Now we have received, not the spirit of the world, but the spirit which is of God; that we might know the things that are freely given to us of God.

Which things also we speak, not in the words which man's wisdom teacheth, but which the Holy Ghost teacheth; comparing spiritual things with spiritual.
1 Corinthians 2:12-13

While it is true that the things of the Spirit (and of the spirit world) are not read to the mind of man - natural man - they are nevertheless real, and discernible. However, God's Word makes it plain that this is only accomplished by spiritual means. The efforts of our natural man are futile.

But the natural man receiveth not the things of the Spirit of God: for they are foolishness unto him: neither can he know them, because they are spiritually discerned.
1 Corinthians 2:14

The same principle applies to the understanding of the spirit world.

Our securtity lie in seeing nothing, recognizing nothing, after the flesh (the natural man); in knowing nothing (spiritually speaking) thereby.

Wherefore henceforth know we no man after the flesh: yea, though we have known Christ after the flesh, yet now henceforth know we him no more.
2 Corinthians 5:16

This is accomplished by the use of the gift of the discerning of spirits: the God-given ability to detect the presence and acertain the identity of spirits, whether they be good or bad.

The gift of the discerning of spirits is not by any means the least of the spiritual abilities. It is the God-given ability to detect the presence and acertain the identity of spirits, whether God who is the Holy Spirit; the spirit of man which is in man; the Spirit of Christ, that new creature in you; one or more of the angels of glory; one or more of the spirits of hell or Satan himself.

We see this gift in operation in John the Baptist, referring to certain people as a generation of vipers: snakes, not sheep.

Then said he to the multitude that came forth to be baptized of him, O generation of vipers, who hath warned you to flee from the wrath to come?
Luke 3:7

John was certainly not addressing their flesh, any more than Jesus was when He declared that those priests in the temple were seed of the serpent.

Jesus called certain Pharisees vipers.

O generation of vipers....Matt. 12:34

On another occasion He did likewise, this time including the appellation "serpents".

Ye serpents, ye generation of vipers...Matt.23:33

When freeing the woman from a spirit of infirmity, (which He discerned,) He was able to declare that Satan himself had bound her with it.

And, behold, there was a woman which had a spirit of infirmity eighteen years, and was bowed together, and could in no wise lift up herself.

And when Jesus saw her, he called her to him, and said unto her, Woman, thou art loosed from thine infirmity.

And he laid his hands on her: and immediately she was made straight, and glorified God.
                              Luke 13:11-13

The ruler of the synagogue objected to this miracle of deliverance on the basis of the fact that it was performed on the sabbath.

And the ruler of the synagogue answered with indignation, because that Jesus had healed on the sabbath day, and said unto the people, there are six days in which men ought to work: in them therefore come and be healed, and not on the sabbath day.

In rebuking him, Jesus shed a bit more light on the operation of this gift of the discerning of spirits, when He said:

The Lord then answered him, and said, Thou hypocrite, doth not each one of you on the sabbath loose his ox or his ass from the stall, and lead him away to watering?

And ought not this woman, being a daughter of Abraham, whom Satan hath bound, lo, these eighteen years, be loosed from this bond on the sabbath day?
                              Luke 13:15-16

His declaration that she was a daughter of Abraham does not mean that He recognized her as a Hebrew lady. Abraham is not the father of Israel; Jacob is. Abraham is the father of them that believe.

Know ye therefore that they which are of faith, the same are the children of Abraham.

Galatians 3:7

He recognized the Spirit of Christ in her. He declared that Satan himself had bound her, utilizing a spirit of infirmity for a bond. All this was accomplished by the operation of the gift of the discering of spirits.

Jesus cured many of their unclean spirits. To do this, He had to detect their presence and ascertain their identity. In other words, His amazing ministry of casting out devils was in itself a testimony to the fact that He walked in the use of the gift of the discerning of spirits.

Peter exercised this gift when he discerned what manner of spirit was motivating Simon of Samaria.

And when Simon saw that through laying on of the apostles' hands the Holy Ghost was given, he offered them money,

Saying, Give me also this power, that on whomsoever I lay hands, he may receive the Holy Ghost.

But Peter said unto him, Thy money perish with thee, because thou hast thought that the gift of God may be purchased with money.

Thou hast neither part nor lot in this matter: for thy heart is not right in the sight of God.

Repent therefore of this thy wickedness, and pray God, if perhaps the thought of thine heart may be forgiven thee.

For I perceive that thou art in the gall of bitterness, and in the bond of iniquity.

Acts 8:18-23

Simon had, by all outward appearances, accepted Christ. Philipa had tacitly accepted the man's profession of faith, and baptized him.

Then Simon himself believéd also: and when he was baptized, he continued with Philip, and wondered, beholding the miracles and signs which were done.

Acts 8:13

Simon, however, experienced no new birth. His was mental asset to divine revelation, mental assent only. This is proven by the word of Peter:

99

Thou hast neither part nor lot in this matter: for thy heart is not right in the sight of God.

Acts 8:21

Note: If a man has really believed on Jesus Christ as a personal Saviour, his heart is right with God

Paul, when dealing with Elyman the sorcerer, utilized the gift of the discerning of spirits.

And when they had gone through the isle unto Paphos, they found a certain sorcerer, a false prophet, a Jew, whose name was Barjesus:

Which was with the deputy of the country, Sergius Paulus, a prudent man; who called for Barnabas and Saul, and desired to hear the word of God.

But Elymas the sorcerer (for so is his name by interpretation) withstood them, seeking to turn away the deputy from the faith.

Then Saul, (who also is called Paul,) filled with the Holy Ghost, set his eyes on him,

And said, O full of all subtilty and all mischief, thou child of the devil, thou enemy of all righteousness, wilt thou not cease to pervert the right ways of the Lord?

And now, behold, the hand of the Lord is upon thee, and thou shalt be blind, not seeing the sun for a season. And immediately there fell on him a mist and a darkness; and he went about seeking some to lead him by the hand.

Acts 13:6-11

Again Paul walked boldly in the use of this gift when delivering the girl possessed by a spirit of divination, in Philippi.

And it came to pass, as we went to prayer, a certain damsel possessed with a spirit of divination met us, which brought her masters much gain by soothsaying:

The same followed Paul and us, and cried, saying, These men are the servants of the most high God, which shew unto us the way of salvation.

And this did she many days. But Paul, being grieved, turned and said to the spirit, I command thee in the name of Jesus Christ to come out of her. And he came out the same hour.

Acts 16:16-18

Note: Do not confuse the discerning of spirits with the act of casting them out. Their presence and identity must, of necessity, be discerning in order that they may be cast out. But discerning the presence and ascertaining the identity of spirits is one thing; the casting out of devils is another thing altogether.

That Timothy possessed the gift of the discerning of spirits is made very evident. The entire fourth chapter of Paul's first letter to him is devoted to the serious condition existing or coming into existence in the church, i.e. doctrines of devils that would be brought in by seducing spirits.

Now the Spirit speaketh expressly, that in the latter times some shall depart from the faith, giving heed to seducing spirits, and doctrines of devils;

Speaking lies in hypocrisy; having their conscience seared with a hot iron;

Forbidding to marry, and commanding to abstain from meats, which God hath created to be received with thanksgiving of them which believe and know the truth.
1 Timothy 4:1-3

Timothy is exhorted not to neglect a certain gift which Paul declares is in him by the laying on of the hands of the Presbytery.

For every creature of God is good, and nothing to be refused, if it be received with thanksgiving:
1 Timothy 4:4

If the context means anything at all, then the gift referred to could only be the gift of the discerning of spirits.

Many people today do not believe in the reality and presence of evil spirits, nor agree with any teachings concerning them. I often wonder what they do with all of the preceeding Scriptures. For that matter, what do they do with all those dealing with **witches, wizards, necromancers, those folk who engage in the black arts**? Here are a few of that very type of Scripture. You will notice the frank, clearly stated facts that these people are engaging in the contacting of various unclean spirits, or are possessed of them, as the case may be, and that the type of spirit contacted or possessing the person is clearly designated.

Regard not them that have familiar spirits, neither seek after wizards, to be defiled by them: I am the LORD your God.
Leviticus 19:31

And the soul that turneth after such as have familiar spirits, and after wizards, to go a whoring after them, I will even set my face against that soul, and will cut him off from among his people.
Leviticus 20:6

When thou art come into the land which the LORD thy God giveth thee, thou shalt not learn to do after the abominations of those nations.

There shall not be found among you any one that maketh his son or his daughter to pass through the fire, or that useth divination, or an observer of times, or an enchanter, or a witch,
Or a charmer, or a consulter with familiar spirits, or a wizard, or a necromancer.
Deuteronomy 18:9-11

I will now draw your attention to a rather misunderstood chapter of the Word of God, a chapter many of God's people would just as well not read. I have even heard a minister of the Gosple, a man of God, refer to this portion of Holy writ as "the spiritists' chapter". My brother, my sister, friend of God, whoever you are reading this book; listen to me. The spiritists have no chapter in the Word of our God. It is our book: every chapter, every verse, every line, every promise, every statement of fact.

We have every right to a thorough understanding of its contents. Therefore let us look into this so-called "spiritists' chapter" now.

Now Samuel was dead, and all Israel had lamented him, and buried him in Ramah, even in his own city. And Saul had put away those that had familiar spirits, and the wizards, out of the land.

And the Philistines gathered themselves together, and came and pitched in Shunem: and Saul gathered all Israel together, and they pitched in Gilboa.

And when Saul saw the host of the Philistines, he was afraid, and his heart greatly trembled.

And when Saul enquired of the LORD, the LORD answered him not, neither by dreams, nor by Urim, nor by prophets.

Then said Saul unto his servants, Seek me a woman that hath a familiar spirit, that I may go to her, and enquire of her. And his servants said to him, Behold, there is a woman that hath a familiar spirit at Endor.

And Saul disguised himself, and put on other raiment, and he went, and two men with him, and they came to the woman by night: and he said, I pray thee, divine unto me by the familiar spirit, and bring me him up, whom I shall name unto thee.

And the woman said unto him, Behold, thou knowest what Saul hath done, how he hath cut off those that have familiar spirits, and the wizards, out of the land: wherefore then layest thou a snare for my life, to cause me to die?

And Saul sware to her by the LORD, saying, As the LORD liveth, there shall no punishment happen to thee for this thing.

Then said the woman, Whom shall I bring up unto thee? And he said, Bring me up Samuel.

And when the woman saw Samuel, she cried with a loud voice: and the woman spake to Saul, saying, Why hast thou deceived me? For thou art Saul.

And the king said unto her, Be not afraid: for what sawest thou? And the woman said unto Saul, I saw gods ascending out of the earth.

And he said unto her, What form is he of? And she said, An old man cometh up; and he is covered with a mantle. And Saul perceived that it was Samuel, and he stooped with his face to the ground, and bowed himself.
1 Samuel 28:3-14

Saul, mighty man of arms, king of Israel and commander-in-chief of her armed forces, was afraid. His enemies were encamped round about him, and, though he sought by every known means for an answer from God, the heavens were brass. The Lord God of Israel would have nothing to do with him.

Having walked with God in the realm of the spirit, he was used to supernatural guidance. Knowing that he must do battles with his mortal enemies on the morrow, he yearned for that supernatural guidance now. Receiving no response from heaven, he turned to the black arts, to spiritism; he sought out a witch, a spiritist medium, and consulted with her. At one time Saul had been zealous for the Lord. In those days he had done away with the witches and wizards in Israel. He had been the terror of the spiritists and necromancers. Now he disguised himself, put on other clothing, and went to this witch in the night, taking two men with him.

....from his shoulders and upward he was higher than any of the people.
1 Samuel 9:2

I am asking you, how could this man disguise himself?

We read of Jeroboam's wife, how she disguised herself so that no one knew she was the queen. This was at the request of her husband, Jeroboam, the king of Israel.

And Jeroboam said to his wife, Arise, I pray thee, and disguise thyself, that thou be not known to be the wife of Jeroboam; and get thee to Shiloh: behold,

there is Ahijah the prophet, which told me that I should be king over this people.

And Jeroboam's wife did so, and arose, and went to Shiloh, and came to the house of Ahijah. But Ahijah could not see; for his eyes were set by reason of his age.

1 Kings 14:4

Yes, even though she was the queen, a well known figure in Israel, she managed so to disguise herself that now one knew who she was; no one.

It's not so difficult a trick if you are an average sized person, average height, average weigt, etc., but Saul stood head and shoulders above the next tallest man in Israel! His actual height is not recorded, but he must have towered upwards to a great height for a man, for Israel was noted for her tall men, and he was head and shoulders above them all.

I am a man of average height. I just measured my head and shoulders:fifteen inches. A man of great height would measure more than this.

Saul must have stood up to at least a foot and half taller than the next tallest man in the whole country! How are you going to disguise a man like that - dress him up as a horse, and have him walk on all four? Perhaps he would disguise better as a dinosaur, maybe a Tyrannosaurus!

Add to this the further fact that he was commander-in-chief of the armed forces of Israel. He was a public figure, a well-known figure. Disguise him? You can have the job. I don't want it.

So this towering hulk of humanity, Saul, king of Israel, disguised himself and came unto the witch of En-dor by night. Now the place where she lived was a cave. This was because Saul had persecuted the witches and wizards unto the death. She escaped death by living and carrying on her nefarious work there.

And Saul disguised himself, and put on other raiment, and he went, and two men with him, and they came to the woman by night: and he said, I pray thee, divine unto me by the familiar spirit, and bring me him up, whom I shall name unto thee.

And the woman said unto him, Behold, thou knowest what Saul hath done, how he hath cut off those that have familiar spirits, and the wizards, out of the land: wherefore then layest thou a snare for my life, to cause me to die?

1 Samuel 28:8-9

Notice that the witch is talking to Saul about Saul. The very fact that the subject of their conversation was the man himself, coupled with his tremendous

104

THE GIFT OF THE DISCERNING OF SPIRITS

height - which was impossible to hide - should have told her who her visitor was. Besides, he had two other men with him. I don't care whether they were the next two tallest men in Israel, the two shortest, or two men of medium height. It matters not what their build, or their height. One thing is certain: their presence would augment his height in her eyes!

No one in Israel had the right, the authority, or the power to take such an oath, or to make such a promise, save the king only. Kings were supreme potentates in those days, and did what they pleased, how they pleased, when they pleased. And this man stands before her and swears to her by the Lord, the God of Israel, that no punishment of any kind shall come upon her for doing what he is asking her to do; and still she does not recognize him.

Then said the woman, Whom shall I bring up unto thee? And he said, Bring me up Samuel.

And when the woman saw Samuel, she cried with a loud voice: and the woman spake to Saul, saying, Why hast thou deceived me? For thou art Saul.
1 Samuel 28:11-12

Oh, Oh! Something has gone wrong! Suddenly the woman is aware of the identity of her visitor.

... Why hast thou deceived me? For thou art Saul.
1 Samuel 28:12

She accused him of deceit, declares his identity, and desires to know why he has deceived her in the matter of his identity? Now she really fears for her life!

But how did she discover him? What woke her up? What gave the show away? How did she know? Because she saw Samuel! Now surely you don't believe that she raised Samuel from the dead! No, I not only do not believe that she raised him from the dead; I know she did not. However I do know that it was Samuel who came up out of the earth.

And when the woman saw Samuel...
1 Samuel 28:12

She did not see his ghost, but Samuel himself. Furthermore, this woman did not recognize Samuel when she saw him. Evidently she had never before laid eyes on him. This is made apparent by the fact that when he now appeared, she did recognize him.

And the king said unto her, Be not afraid: for what sawest thou? And the woman said unto Saul, I saw gods ascending out of the earth.

105

And he said unto her, What form is he of? And she said, An old man cometh up; and he is covered with a mantle. And Saul perceived that it was Samuel, and he stooped with his face to the ground, and bowed himself.
1 Samuel 28:13-14

Now, why was she afraid when she saw Samuel, whom she did not recognize? Why was she so fearful when Samuel arose? Why did this woman - who made her living by (supposedly) contacting the dead fear in the presence of reality? Because she had never contacted in all her born days. The dead are dead.

..a living dog is better than a dead lion.

For the living know that they shall die: but the dead know not any thing, neither have they any more a reward; for the memory of them is forgotten.

Also their love, and their hatred, and their envy, is now perished; neither have they any more a portion for ever in any thing that is done under the sun.
Ecclesiastes 9:4-6

Certain religious dogmas of certain religious groups teach the communion with the dead. A great deal of this is taught under the guise of prayer. A person, dead is declared a saint, but God's Word looks after this matter.

Call now, if there be any that will answer thee; and to which of the saints wilt thou turn?
Job 5:1

Necromancers graft on love: your love for a departed sweetheart, mother, dad, wife, husband, son, or daughter. They claim to be in contact with them, and to receive messages from them for you. Such claims are false, and to put one's confidence in them is wrong, absolutely wrong.

The witch of En-dor was all wrong too, and everything was going to the contrary this day. She was not expecting Samuel to rise, neither did she raise him! She was the most astonished and frightened woman in the whole wide world when it happened. But she had expected something, or was it someone? Yes, she had expected the usual spirits vistitation. She had expected the usual manifestations, whatever the particular manifestations were of the spirit which possessed her. She expected her familiar spirit to manifest himself and put on a show, as usual. But that spirit was now hiding in the bowels of hell for fear of Samuel, who was raised from the dead.

.... And Saul perceived that it was Samuel.
1 Samuel 28:14

106

And Samuel said to Saul, Why hast thou disquieted me, to bring me up?
1 Samuel 28:15

The witch never raised him. She had never raised anyone, nor contacted any of the dead on behalf of anyone, in her entire life. No witch, wizard, spiritist or necromancer of any kind ever does.

And every spirit that confesseth not that Jesus Christ is come in the flesh is not of God: and this is that spirit of antichrist, whereof ye have heard that it should come; and even now already is it in the world.
1 John 4:3

For ye have not received the spirit of bondage again to fear; but ye have received the Spirit of adoption, whereby we cry, Abba, Father.
Romans 8:15

We are of God: he that knoweth God heareth us; he that is not of God heareth not us. Hereby know we the spirit of truth, and the spirit of error.
1 John 4:6

For God hath not given us the spirit of fear; but of power, and of love, and of a sound mind.
2 Timothy 1:7

And the spirit of jealousy come upon him, and he be jealous of his wife, and she be defiled: or if the spirit of jealousy come upon him, and he be jealous of his wife, and she be not defiled:
Numbers 5:14

My people ask counsel at their stocks, and their staff declareth unto them: for the spirit of whoredoms hath caused them to err, and they have gone a whoring from under their God.
Hosea 4:12

They will not frame their doings to turn unto their God: for the spirit of whoredoms is in the midst of them, and they have not known the LORD.
Hosea 5:4

(According as it is written, God hath given them the spirit of slumber, eyes that they should not see, and ears that they should not hear;) unto this day.
Romans 11:8

The LORD hath mingled a perverse spirit in the midst thereof: and they have caused Egypt to err in every work thereof, as a drunken man staggereth in his vomit.
Isaiah 19:14

There are multitudes of evil spirits whose names - designatory titles - are not listed in the Word of God. There are spirits of emulation and strife, sensual spirits, suicidal spirits, spirits of depression, hallucination and obsession. There are morbid spirits, sullen spirits, sadistic spirits, various kinds of spirits of insantity, oppression, fixation etc. There is a fallacious spirit. There are lying spirits, deceiving spirits, many kinds of unclean spirits. These all make their abode in the minds of men.

If I could open your cranial structure or handle your brain without injuring or destroying you, I could control your every move, your speech, even your thought life.

Thank God we cannot do this to each other. However, spirits do just that. They enter the mind and take control of the person that they possess. More than one spirit of infirmity operates after this fashion, taking possession of the cranial structure in its entirety, and from there controlling the whole body, its motions, etc,

Dr. Luke understood that epilepsy is caused by a spirit called "Epilepsy."

And it came to pass, that on the next day, when they were come down from the hill, much people met him.

And, behold, a man of the company cried out, saying, Master, I beseech thee, look upon my son: for he is mine only child.

And, lo, a spirit taketh him, and he suddenly crieth out; and it teareth him that he foameth again, and bruising him hardly departeth from him.

And I besought thy disciples to cast him out; and they could not.

And Jesus answering said, O faithless and perverse generation, how long shall I be with you, and suffer you? Bring thy son hither.

And as he was yet a coming, the devil threw him down, and tare him. And Jesus rebuked the unclean spirit, and healed the child, and delivered him again to his father.

Luke 9:37-42

The manifestations of the spirit of man are to be seen clearly all about us. The manifestations of the spirits of hell are as clearly traceable. The manifestations of the Holy Spirit are listed for our benefit in the Word of God.

But the manifestation of the Spirit is given to every man to profit withal.

For to one is given by the Spirit the word of wisdom; to another the word of knowledge by the same Spirit;

To another faith by the same Spirit; to another the gifts of healing by the same Spirit;

To another the working of miracles; to another prophecy; to another discerning of spirits; to another divers kinds of tongues; to another the interpretation of tongues:

But all these worketh that one and the selfsame Spirit, dividing to every man severally as he will.

For as the body is one, and hath many members, and all the members of that one body, being many, are one body: so also is Christ.

1 Corinthians 12:7-12

These are, of cause, the product of the deliberate operation of the gifts of the Spirit.

But God hath revealed them unto us by his Spirit: for the Spirit searcheth all things, yea, the deep things of God.

1 Corinthians 2:10

But the Comforter, which is the Holy Ghost, whom the Father will send in my name, he shall teach you all things, and bring all things to your remembrance, whatsoever I have said unto you.

John 14:26

Howbeit when he, the Spirit of truth, is come, he will guide you into all truth: for he shall not speak of himself; but whatsoever he shall hear, that shall he speak: and he will shew you things to come.

He shall glorify me: for he shall receive of mine, and shall shew it unto you.

All things that the Father hath are mine: therefore said I, that he shall take of mine, and shall shew it unto you.

John 16:13-15

It is our spiritual man (the new creature) who receives enlightenment regarding spiritual verities, even as it is the new creature who receives the gifts of the spirit.

Now we have received, not the spirit of the world, but the spirit which is of God; that we might know the things that are freely given to us of God.

I Cor. 2:12

Our natural man (the spirit of man which is in man) does not receive the things of the Spirit of God.

But the natural man receiveth not the things of the Spirit of God: for they are foolishness unto him: neither can he know them, because they are spiritually discerned.

1 Corinthians 2:1

Of all the armament we may possess in Christ, none is so essential to the well-being of the Church as the gift of discerning of spirits. It consitutes the eyes of the Church in the realm of the spirit. Being a gift, it cannot be purchased or earned. You receive it by faith, as you receive anything else from God.

Timothy received the gift of the discerning of spirits by prophecy with the laying on of the hands of the presbytery. In other words, inspired utterance declared this gift in him at the time of his ordination. Paul wrote to him that he should not fail to utilize this amazing supernatural ability.

Neglect not the gift that is in thee, which was given thee by prophecy, with the laying on of the hands of the presbytery.

1 Timothy 4:14

That Paul referred here to the gift of the discerning of spirits is made evident by the context.

Some people refer to the gifts of the spirit as **spirits**. This is error born of lack of knowledge. In the Old Testament, the phrase utilized to denote any of these supernatural abilities is "the spirit of ". (For example, "the spirit of wisdom", this signifying the gift of the word of wisdom as it is referred to in the New Testament language.)

They are not **spirits,** but gifts, gifts of one Spirit, the Spirit of the living God.

Peter refers to a supernatural ability as

... the ability which God giveth

1 Peter 4:11B

Some refer to the **fruit** of the Spirit as the **spirits.** Wrong again! These are **fruit,** not **spirits.** They are the fruit of one Spirit; the Holy Spirit.

But the fruit of the Spirit is love, joy, peace, longsuffering, gentleness, goodness, faith,

Meekness, temperance: against such there is no law.

Galatians 5:22-23

These should manifest in the life of every Christian.

Others refer to the works of the flesh as **spirits**. Again they are wrong! These are **works; not gifts, not fruit, not spirits, not even the works of spirits.**

These are the works of the flesh, the works of the natural (our natural) man.

> Now the works of the flesh are manifest, which are these; Adultery, fornication, uncleanness, lasciviousness,
>
> Idolatry, witchcraft, hatred, variance, emulations, wrath, strife, seditions, heresies,
>
> Envyings, murders, drunkenness, revellings, and such like: of the which I tell you before, as I have also told you in time past, that they which do such things shall not inherit the kingdom of God.
> Galatians 5:19-21

God has not left us at the mercy of Satan. However, we could allow Satan to take advantage of us:

> Lest Satan should get an advantage of us: for we are not ignorant of his devices.
> 2 Corinthians 2:11

He encourages us to put the spirits of hell on the spot, as it were.

> Beloved, believe not every spirit, but try the spirits whether they are of God...
> 1 John 4:1A

There are certain things which neither a spirit of hell nor the spirit of man can do. Hereby know ye the Spirit of God:

> Hereby know ye the Spirit of God: Every spirit that confesseth that Jesus Christ is come in the flesh is of God:
>
> And every spirit that confesseth not that Jesus Christ is come in the flesh is not of God: and this is that spirit of antichrist, whereof ye have heard that it should come; and even now already is it in the world.
> 1 John 4:2-3

In this Scripture portion it is made very apparent that no spirit of hell will admit that Jesus Christ is come in the flesh. Likewise, any spirit that is in harmony with heaven will readily admit this truth.

111

Wherefore I give you to understand, that no man speaking by the Spirit of God calleth Jesus accursed: and that no man can say that Jesus is the Lord, but by the Holy Ghost.

1 Corinthians 12:3

In this verse we learn that if any man, purportedly speaking via the operation of the utterance gifts of the spirit, calls Jesus accursed from God, and brands Him a sinner, or an inpostor, this man is not doing what he professes he is doing.

This man is not speaking via the use of the utterance gifts, for it is impossible for any one, while doing so, to speak against Christ. By the same token, we learn here that if any man calls Him Lord, while purporting to be speaking via the operation of spiritual gifts, this man is speaking the truth.

Such an individual is not speaking the ramblings of the human spirit, neither is he possessed and driven by an evil spirit. He is speaking by the Spirit of God, which is in him. Remember the word of Balaam:

If Balak would give me his house full of silver and gold, I cannot go beyond the commandment of the LORD, to do either good or bad of mine own mind; but what the LORD saith, that will I speak?

Numbers 24:13

This man knew that if he stuck to the use of utterance gifts of the Spirit, he could not give voice to his own opinions, desires, secret ambitions, etc. This is confirmed in Luke's account of the day of Pentecost:

... we do hear them speak in our tongues the wonderful works of God.

Acts 2:11

Besides leaving us explicit instructions regarding the trying of the spirits, God has left us spiritual weapons of warfare, whereby we have been made able to cope with the enemies, the spirits of hell. The most necessary weapon in this field of endeavor is, of cause, the gift of the discerning of spirits: that God-given ability to detect the presence and ascertain the identity of spirits.

As with all the gifts of the spirit, the gift of the discerning of spirits is a God-given ability which you operate at your own - entirely at your own will.

As every man hath received the gift, even so minister the same...

... if any man minister, let him do it as of the ability which God giveth...

1 Peter 4:10A-11B

112

But strong meat belongeth to them that are of full age, even those who by reason of use have their senses exercised to discern both good and evil.
Hebrews 5:14

Then shall ye return, and discern between the righteous and the wicked, between him that serveth God and him that serveth him not.
Malachi 3:18

PART THREE

THE POWER GIFTS OF THE SPIRIT

PRELIMINARY

The third and last group of the supernatural abilities (i.e., the power gifts of the Spirit) are so called because they operate by the power of God. This is the power in and by which Paul preached the gospel to the heathen and wrought the signs which confirmed it to their hearts.

For I will not dare to speak of any of those things which Christ hath not wrought by me, to make the Gentiles obedient, by word and deed,

Through mighty signs and wonders, by the power of the Spirit of God; so that from Jerusalem, and round about unto Illyricum, I have fully preached the gospel of Christ.
Romans 15:18-19

Paul declares that it was according to the effectual working of God's power that he was made a minister of the gospel of God's grace.

Whereof I was made a minister, according to the gift of the grace of God given unto me by the effectual working of his power.
Ephesians 3:7

He likewise declares that while God is able to do exceeding abundantly on our behalf, yet it is according to His power working in us.

Now unto him that is able to do exceeding abundantly above all that we ask or think, according to the power that worketh in us,
Ephesians 3:20

Paul states further that the work of the ministry will only be accomplished by that which every child of God contributes in the supernatural realm. He makes it very plain that this is supplied according to the effectiveness of the working of the power of God in us.

From whom the whole body fitly joined together and compacted by that which every joint supplieth, according to the effectual working in the measure of every part, maketh increase of the body unto the edifying of itself in love.
Ephesians 4:16

We can readily see here the need for the gifts of the Spirit. However, we see also that without the power of God in us, and our effectual use of it, we will never accomplish that which God has planned for us to accomplish. Jesus promised that we should have that power after we were baptized with the Holy Ghost.

But ye shall receive power, after that the Holy Ghost is come upon you: and ye shall be witnesses unto me both in Jerusalem, and in all Judaea, and in Samaria, and unto the uttermost part of the earth.
Acts 1:8

Once we have received this power, it is in us.

But we have this treasure in earthen vessels, that the excellency of the power may be of God, and not of us.
2 Corinthians 4:7

This power (this tresure) is necessary for the effective operation of the third group of the supernatural abilities. For this reason they are commonly referred to as the **power gifts of the Spirit.**

This group of spiritual gifts are also called **impartation gifts**. This is because by your deliberate operation of them you impart something to others, or, (putting it another way), something goes out from you to others. When the woman with the issue of blood touched Jesus and was instantly healed, He said:

...I perceive that virtue is gone out of me. Luke 8:46B

Another time, Jesus was ministering in a great plain, and multitudes came to hear Him, and to be healed of their infirmities.

And the whole multitude sought to touch him: for there went virtue out of him, and healed them all.
Luke 6:19

When Peter and John stood facing the need of the cripple who spent his time begging at the Beautiful Gate of the Temple in Jerusalem, Peter said;

... such as I have give I thee. Acts 3:6B

Here we have a concrete case of a man of God imparting something, something he possessed, to another. That this was something which met the need of the recipient (Who never had walked) enabling him to leap to his feet and walk, is made evident by the content.

And he took him by the right hand, and lifted him up: and immediately his feet and ankle bones received strength.

And he leaping up stood, and walked, and entered with them into the temple, walking, and leaping, and praising God.
Acts 3:7-8

Incidentally, Peter is the sacred writer who wrote:

If any man speak, let him speak as the oracles of God; if any man minister, let him do it as of the ability which God giveth: that God in all things may be glorified through Jesus Christ, to whom be praise and dominion for ever and ever. Amen.
1 Peter 4:11

The ability given to us of God are the gifts of the Spirit, and it is evident that in this quotation Peter is referring to the **power or impartation gifts of the Spirit.**

These power or impartation gifts of the Spirit are three in number. We list them here in their proper sequence or order.

POWER OR IMPARTATION GIFTS:

1. The gift of **Faith.**
2. The gift of **Healing**.
3. The gift of the performing of **Miracles.**

We shall study them in this, their proper order.

CHAPTER SEVEN

THE GIFT OF FAITH

But without faith it is impossible to please him: for he that cometh to God must believe that he is, and that he is a rewarder of them that diligently seek him.
Hebrews 11:6

WHAT IT IS NOT

The gift of faith is not a different faith, another kind of faith. To say so is to manifest the grossest type of ignorance. Faith is faith; faith is substance; faith is evidence.

Now faith is the substance of things hoped for, the evidence of things not seen.
Hebrews 11:1

Faith is belief, which when acted upon to receive from God, becomes the evidence of that which you have not received as yet. Yes, faith is the substance and likewise the evidence; but we are not studying these. We are studying an ability; a supernatural ability; the ability to do certain specific things with that substance, thereby producing the evidence.

WHAT IT IS

The gift of faith, one of the nine gifts of the spirit, is the God-given ability to believe for the fantastically impossible to come to pass (and that at your word,) and the further ability to impart faith to others.

BELIEVE FOR THE IMPOSSIBLE TO COME TO PASS

We see this gift in this phase of its operations in the ministry of Jesus Himself when He cursed the fig tree.

And on the morrow, when they were come from Bethany, he was hungry:

And seeing a fig tree afar off having leaves, he came, if haply he might find any thing thereon: and when he came to it, he found nothing but leaves; for the time of figs was not yet.

And Jesus answered and said unto it, No man eat fruit of thee hereafter for ever. And his disciples heard it.
Mark 11:12-14

The next morning Peter noticed that the tree was dead, dried up from the roots. He drew Christ's attention to this phenomenon.

And Jesus answering saith unto them, Have faith in God.

For verily I say unto you, That whosoever shall say unto this mountain, Be thou removed, and be thou cast into the sea; and shall not doubt in his heart, but shall believe that those things which he saith shall come to pass; he shall have whatsoever he saith.

Mark 11:22-23

Now let us take a closer look at the latter part of that answer, reviewing it statement by statement:

1. *Whosever shall say unto this mountain,* Christ taught, in this phrase, that we should address ourselves to the problem, to the need rather than to God with reference to the need.

2. *Be thou removed.* Here we have the command. It goes without saying, that what Christ was placing before us here was authority, our authority in Him. We are authorized to command. The implied thought is, of course, that our commands shall be obeyed.

3. *And shall not doubt in his heart.* There is no place for doubt in the economy of God. To doubt is to create rebellion within the heart of that one unto whom the command is addressed. Whatever we accomplish in Christ Jesus, is accomplished by faith. We accomplish nothing otherwise or by any other means. Doubt is the opposite of faith. To doubt, therefore, would be to war against one's own effort. Thus the one issuing the command would defeat his own purpose.

4. *But shall believe that those things which he saith shall come to pass;* To successfully command demands with the heart of the one issuing the command implicit faith that the word spoken shall be obeyed. That which we are within, is manifest by that which proceeds from our lips. This embraces more, much more than the phrases employed. The manner in which our command is issued, the tone of voice, inflection, accompanying gestures etc., all speak loudly our implicit faith in the fact that we expect our command to be fulfilled, or betray our doubt that it will be.

5. *He shall have whatever he saith.* The man who produces the result, is that man who, banishing all doubt from his inward parts, believes that without equivocation, every command he issues shall be obeyed, and to the letter.

That Christ is referring to the exercise of the gift of faith is made evident by the following from the pen of Paul.

**... though I have all faith, so that I could remove mountains,
I Corinthians 13:2C**

The context proves that Paul was speaking about the gift of faith. The mountain-moving infers this.

On one occasion, Christ's chosen ones, the twelve, asked Him for a larger portion of faith. His reply was a confirmation of all the foregoing. And the Apostles said unto the Lord, "increase our faith".

And the apostles said unto the Lord, Increase our faith.

And the Lord said, If ye had faith as a grain of mustard seed, ye might say unto this sycamine tree, Be thou plucked up by the root, and be thou planted in the sea; and it should obey you.
                                        Luke 17:5-6

And Jesus, in another place, said unto them:

And Jesus said unto them, Because of your unbelief: for verily I say unto you, If ye have faith as a grain of mustard seed, ye shall say unto this mountain, Remove hence to yonder place; and it shall remove; and nothing shall be impossible unto you.
                                        Matthew 17:20

Jesus not only utilized the gift of faith in its first or primal phase when He cursed the fig tree; He taught His disciples how to do likewise. There is no doubt that they learned their lesson well. Even a casual study of their lives and ministries will make that evident.

The Word of God implies that Barnabas possessed this gift of faith.

Then tidings of these things came unto the ears of the church which was in Jerusalem: and they sent forth Barnabas, that he should go as far as Antioch.

Who, when he came, and had seen the grace of God, was glad, and exhorted them all, that with purpose of heart they would cleave unto the Lord.

For he was a good man, and full of the Holy Ghost and of faith: and much people was added unto the Lord.
                                        Acts 11:22-24

In Paul's second letter to Timothy he exhorts him to stir up a gift of the Spirit which he says is in him by the laying on of his hands.

Wherefore I put thee in remembrance that thou stir up the gift of God, which is in thee by the putting on of my hands.
                                                                    II Timothy 1:6

A study of the context proves that this could be nothing less than the gift of faith.

When I call to remembrance the unfeigned faith that is in thee, which dwelt first in thy grandmother Lois, and thy mother Eunice; and I am persuaded that in thee also.
                                                                    II Timothy 1:5

When Peter and John healed the crippled at the temple gate in the city of Jerusalem, the use of the gift of faith in this phase of its operations is very evident.

In the name of Jesus Christ of Nazareth rise up and walk.
                                                                    Acts 3:6c

No praying, no begging, no supplicating, here! Peter commands in the name of the Lord, and the work is done. Note the similarity between his handling of this case and Christ's commanding of the fig tree.

Another case of a man of God utilizing this amazing God-given ability is that of Joshua extending the day.

Then spake Joshua to the LORD in the day when the LORD delivered up the Amorites before the children of Israel, and he said in the sight of Israel, Sun, stand thou still upon Gibeon; and thou, Moon, in the valley of Ajalon.

And the sun stood still, and the moon stayed, until the people had avenged themselves upon their enemies. Is not this written in the book of Jasher? So the sun stood still in the midst of heaven, and hasted not to go down about a whole day.

And there was no day like that before it or after it, that the LORD hearkened unto the voice of a man: for the LORD fought for Israel.
                                                                    Joshua 10:12-14

Here again we find, not a cringing supplicant, but a man, a man of God; a man led of God, inspired by the Almighty, and acting upon the inspiration of the Almighty, commanding -- and the thing coming to pass at his word. Compare his action with what Jesus taught concerning the exercise of the gift of faith.

For verily I say unto you, That whosoever shall say unto this mountain, Be thou removed, and be thou cast into the sea; and shall not doubt in his heart,

but shall believe that those things which he saith shall come to pass; he shall have whatsoever he saith.

Mark 11:23

Now let us put the two texts together.

Whosoever shall say unto the sun, and to the moon, sun, stand thou still upon Gibeon; and thou, Moon, in the valley of Ajalon; and shall not doubt in his heart, but shall believe that those things which he saith shall come to pass; he shall have whatsoever he saith.

The two texts fit together like a hand and glove. For the one is the instruction; the other is the instruction acted upon.

The Church is always clamoring about the need of Joshua today. That is not the need of the hour. The need is an obedience to the Word. Try walking in Joshua's obedience to this portion of God's Word and see for yourself what I mean.

And, behold, a woman, which was diseased with an issue of blood twelve years, came behind him, and touched the hem of his garment:

For she said within herself, If I may but touch his garment, I shall be whole.

But Jesus turned him about, and when he saw her, he said, Daughter, be of good comfort; thy faith hath made thee whole. And the woman was made whole from that hour.

Matthew 9:20-22

That this woman was exercising the gift of faith, as Jesus taught we should use it, there can be no doubt. She said:

For she said within herself, If I may but touch his garment, I shall be whole.

Matthew 9:21

She touched Him. She received, and Jesus said unto her:

But Jesus turned him about, and when he saw her, he said, Daughter, be of good comfort; thy faith hath made thee whole. And the woman was made whole from that hour.

Matthew 9:22

The result was, of course, the same as with Jesus and the fig tree, Joshua and the sun and the moon, and Peter and the cripple. She saw her very desire come to pass. She made a statement and saw it fulfilled. She was a miracle of deliverance and healing.

The Roman centurion who came to Jesus Christ on behalf of his servant is another outstanding case of a man walking in the use of this supernatural ability.

And when Jesus was entered into Capernaum, there came unto him a centurion, beseeching him,

And saying, Lord, my servant lieth at home sick of the palsy, grievously tormented.

And Jesus saith unto him, I will come and heal him.

The centurion answered and said, Lord, I am not worthy that thou shouldest come under my roof: but speak the word only, and my servant shall be healed.

For I am a man under authority, having soldiers under me: and I say to this man, Go, and he goeth; and to another, Come, and he cometh; and to my servant, Do this, and he doeth it.

When Jesus heard it, he marvelled, and said to them that followed, Verily I say unto you, I have not found so great faith, no, not in Israel.
Matthew 8:5-10

Note that this man said:

... speak the word only, and my servant shall be healed
Matthew 8:8B

Note the result:

And his servant was healed in the self-same hour.
Matthew 8:13B

Another man who veritably shone in his use of this remarkable spiritual ability was Jairus, ruler of the synagogue in Christ's own city:

While he spake these things unto them, behold, there came a certain ruler, and worshipped him, saying, My daughter is even now dead: but come and lay thy hand upon her, and she shall live.
Matthew 9:18

It is Mark who tells us who this man was:

And, behold, there cometh one of the rulers of the synagogue, Jairus by name; and when he saw him, he fell at his feet,
Mark 5:22

124

It was Jesus who did the miracle.

While he yet spake, there came from the ruler of the synagogue's house certain which said, Thy daughter is dead: why troublest thou the Master any further?

As soon as Jesus heard the word that was spoken, he saith unto the ruler of the synagogue, Be not afraid, only believe.

And he suffered no man to follow him, save Peter, and James, and John the brother of James.

And he cometh to the house of the ruler of the synagogue, and seeth the tumult, and them that wept and wailed greatly.

And when he was come in, he saith unto them, Why make ye this ado, and weep? The damsel is not dead, but sleepeth.

And they laughed him to scorn. But when he had put them all out, he taketh the father and the mother of the damsel, and them that were with him, and entereth in where the damsel was lying.

And he took the damsel by the hand, and said unto her, Talitha cumi; which is, being interpreted, Damsel, I say unto thee, arise.

And straightway the damsel arose, and walked; for she was of the age of twelve years. And they were astonished with a great astonishment.
Mark 5:35-42

But it was Jairus who, by the exercise of the gift of faith, caused it all to come to pass. Let us look at the text once again.

While he spake these things unto them, behold, there came a certain ruler, and worshipped him, saying, My daughter is even now dead: but come and lay thy hand upon her, and she shall live.
Matthew 9:18

No begging, or pleading, no "if" ! A clear-cut statement of fact! You do this, and such and such will be the net result.

I would like to also draw to your attention the fact, so evident in each case we studied relative to this matter, that without exception, each believed implicitly that what he had declared would come to pass.

Time would fail us to write of others who wrought works of righteousness, subduing kingdoms of men and devil, and obtaining deliverance, by the use of this mighty gift of the Holy Ghost, the gift of faith, in the first phase of its operations.

IMPARTING FAITH TO OTHERS

This phase of the operation of the gift of faith we see in the ministry of Jesus Christ as He helped the father of the devil-possessed boy to believe.

Jesus had just been on the mount of transfiguration. He had taken with Him only three of His disciples; the other nine waited at the foot of the mount. As He and the three came down the slope on their return, they were met by a huge throng.

And when he came to his disciples, he saw a great multitude about them, and the scribes questioning with them.

And straightway all the people, when they beheld him, were greatly amazed, and running to him saluted him.

And he asked the scribes, What question ye with them?
Mark 9:14-16

They answered Him not, and I am sure that I know why.

And one of the multitude answered and said, Master, I have brought unto thee my son, which hath a dumb spirit;

And wheresoever he taketh him, he teareth him: and he foameth, and gnasheth with his teeth, and pineth away: and I spake to thy disciples that they should cast him out; and they could not.
Mark 9:17-18

Here is a man who is in no condition to receive anything from God. Like all who are not on the ball spiritually, he immediately places the blame upon the other fellow.

... they (your disciples) could not.
Mark 9:18

Jesus rebuked this man. He did not rebuke His disciples. The Scribes and the Pharisees had done that already. Jesus addresses His scathing remarks to the man, the father of the boy.

He answereth him, and saith, O faithless generation, how long shall I be with you? How long shall I suffer you? Bring him unto me.
Mark 9:19

They brought the boy to Christ, and even as the were bringing him the spirit threw him to the ground in another attempt to destroy him.

126

And they brought him unto him: and when he saw him, straightway the spirit tare him; and he fell on the ground, and wallowed foaming.
Mark 9:20

Now Christ entered the battle in earnest. (He) needed not that any should testify of Him:

And needed not that any should testify of man: for he knew what was in man.
John 2:25

Yet you find Him asking this man to tell Him about His son, and about the spirit visitation also. Why? To get the father to talk, of course! Only in this way could He get him to speak the true language of his heart. Only in this way could He cause the man to see his own need, which was greater than his son's, and which made it impossible for anyone to minister successfully in this case. Only by causing him to speak his own state could the man be brought to the place where he could be helped out of his unbelieving condition. He did. Men always do, if given the opportunity.

... out of the abundance of the heart the mouth speaketh.
Matthew 12:34C

And he asked his father, How long is it ago since this came unto him? And he said, Of a child.

And ofttimes it hath cast him into the fire, and into the waters, to destroy him: but if thou canst do any thing, have compassion on us, and help us.
Mark 9:21-22

IF! This man was talking to Jesus. IF? The man was in insulting Deity! "If" you can do anything. The very idea! Jesus took that "if", and bending it like a horseshoe, He placed it where it belonged: around the neck and shoulders of the father of the boy, the man himself.

Jesus said unto him, If thou canst believe, all things are possible to him that believeth.
Mark 9:23

And the fight was won. Christ had pierced the armour of this man's heart and soul. He cried aloud:

Lord, I believe; help thou mine unbelief.
Mark 9:24C

Here Christ, by the operation of the gift of faith, lifted the man, inspirited him, inculcated into him the faith that was lacking, got him to declare himself. We too must work on those to whom we minister. It is absolutely essential that the person coming for help be placed upon believing ground.

There is no gift given which takes away from the needy party the necessity for the exercise of faith. Miracles are not produced by good oratory voices. Neither do preachers carry them about in their briefcases. Miracles are born of the mutual faith of both the person ministering and the party being ministered to. Paul, writing to the Romans, said:

> **For I long to see you, that I may impart unto you some spiritual gift, to the end ye may be established;**
>
> **That is, that I may be comforted together with you by the mutual faith both of you and me.**
>
> **Romans 1:11-12**

A certain nobleman came to Jesus for help for his son who was sick.

> **So Jesus came again into Cana of Galilee, where he made the water wine. And there was a certain nobleman, whose son was sick at Capernaum.**
>
> **When he heard that Jesus was come out of Judaea into Galilee, he went unto him, and besought him that he would come down, and heal his son: for he was at the point of death.**
>
> **John 4:46-47**

This man had ridden a great distance to reach Christ with his request. Notice how he approached Him for the help he needed. He besought Him. Take particular notice of the substance of his request: he desired Christ to make that long journey to Capernaum right now, right in middle of a meeting, whilst ministering to an attentive and needy people.

To the average Christian of today, this marks the nobleman as a shining example of faith. He is a real seeker. True, but is that faith? Does faith supplicate, or state the simple facts of the case? Does faith beg or request? He beseeches Christ to come to Capernaum and heal his son. In the first place he shows no consideration for the multitudes needing Christ right there at the service. In the second place he has absolutely no consideration for Jesus, whom he is asking to make that long ride. In the third place his beseeching declares his lack of faith. Those who believe do not spend the life-long day wringing their hands and pleading with the Almighty as though He were of such a nature as to enjoy watching His children squirm before Him, cringing in subservient supplication for that which He has promised to give to them upon request. Our God is not a sadist. Jesus read this man like a book.

Then said Jesus unto him, Except ye see signs and wonders, ye will not believe.
John 4:48

He would never believe until he saw a miracle; and healings are not produced that way.

But without faith it is impossible to please him: for he that cometh to God must believe that he is, and that he is a rewarder of them that diligently seek him.
Hebrews 11:6

The law of faith has not been altered. The principle upon which it operates is the same today as it has been from the beginning.

Therefore I say unto you, What things soever ye desire, when ye pray, believe that ye receive them, and ye shall have them.
Mark 11:24

The nobleman's first response was nothing more nor less than a manifestation of his lack of faith.

Sir, come down ere my child die.
John 4:49B

Jesus put him on the spot; He brought him to the point where, in sixty seconds of time, he must make a decision.

Go thy way; thy son liveth.
John 4:50A

Now the man was faced with the necessity and the responsibility of saying yes or no to Jesus Christ. He had to act. He either had to dismount and declare his determination to remain until Christ could and would leave with him for Capernaum, or to turn his horse about in obedience to the command of the son of God, and start for home. Jesus left him no middle ground.

The nobleman from Capernaum was different. Then and there he made his decision; he turned his horse about and started the long ride home. Jesus had laid the axe to the root of his problem. He had inculcated into his heart the faith which made Jesus the man of God that He was. The result? The man's son was made whole from that very hour.

Jesus saith unto him, Go thy way; thy son liveth. And the man believed the word that Jesus had spoken unto him, and he went his way.

And as he was now going down, his servants met him, and told him, saying, Thy son liveth.

Then enquired he of them the hour when he began to amend. And they said unto him, Yesterday at the seventh hour the fever left him.

So the father knew that it was at the same hour, in the which Jesus said unto him, Thy son liveth: and himself believed, and his whole house.
John 4:50-53

Two blind men followed Jesus into the house. Their need? Healing; they desired sight.

And when Jesus departed thence, two blind men followed him, crying, and saying, Thou Son of David, have mercy on us.

And when he was come into the house, the blind men came to him: and Jesus saith unto them, Believe ye that I am able to do this? They said unto him, Yea, Lord.
Matthew 9:27-28

And upon the basis of their response we read that they received.

Then touched he their eyes, saying, According to your faith be it unto you. And their eyes were opened; and Jesus straitly charged them, saying, See that no man know it.
Matthew 9:29-30

Jesus lifted their faith by causing them to declare themselves. There was the cripple healed by Peter and John at the temple gate.

Now Peter and John went up together into the temple at the hour of prayer, being the ninth hour.

And a certain man lame from his mother's womb was carried, whom they laid daily at the gate of the temple which is called Beautiful, to ask alms of them that entered into the temple;

Who seeing Peter and John about to go into the temple asked an alms.

And Peter, fastening his eyes upon him with John, said, Look on us.

And he gave heed unto them, expecting to receive something of them.

Then Peter said, Silver and gold have I none; but such as I have give I thee: In the name of Jesus Christ of Nazareth rise up and walk.

And he took him by the right hand, and lifted him up: and immediately his feet and ankle bones received strength.

And he leaping up stood, and walked, and entered with them into the temple, walking, and leaping, and praising God.
Acts 3:1-8

The man asked for alms. Peter and John responded: "Look on us."

They got this man to expect to receive something, and to expect to receive it of them. This is how they brought him on to believing ground. This is why he became a miracle of healing.
Acts 3:4B

Regarding this phase of the operation of the gift of faith, we might well say that without it thus in operation in one's life and ministry, there would be little to show for one's labours at the end of the road. The true purpose behind all preaching, every miracle performed, every devil cast out, behind every healing, is that faith might be inculcated into human hearts that hear and see.

What you possess, you bestow. You cannot give out that which is not in you. Paul declared that this gift was in Timothy by his ministry, i.e., by the putting on of his (Paul's) hands.

Wherefore I put thee in remembrance that thou stir up the gift of God, which is in thee by the putting on of my hands.
Acts 3:4B

There must have been some inspired utterance that went forth out of the mouth of Paul at this time. Otherwise, there would be no sense in Paul writing to Timothy, in this fashion, for neither he, Timothy, nor anyone else would know to which gift he was referring!

It can be made manifest to you that you possess this gift. This can be done (it may be) by inspired utterance when hands are laid upon you. You can know by its presence in you being manifested, i.e., by the fact that you are able to believe for the fantastically impossible to come to pass, and by the fact that you are able to inculcate into the hearts of others that same ability to believe for things unheard of to come to pass at your word.

Now faith is the substance of things hoped for, the evidence of things not seen.
Hebrews 11:1

But without faith it is impossible to please him: for he that cometh to God must believe that he is, and that he is a rewarder of them that diligently seek him.
Hebrews 11:6

Wherefore I put thee in remembrance that thou stir up the gift of God, which is in thee by the putting on of my hands.

II Timothy 1:6

CHAPTER EIGHT

THE GIFT OF HEALING

.... they shall lay hands on the sick, and they shall recover.
Mark 16:18c

WHAT IT IS NOT

It is not a Midas touch. That is, there is no such thing as a gift that makes possible for one to heal others automatically, as though one were a healing machine. Faith is always to be reckoned with.

... without faith it is impossible to please him (God).
Hebrews 11:6

It is not a sensation, nor a sign, in the hand or in any other part of the body.

It is not a ministry of healing. We are studying a gift, not a ministry.

It is not a gift of healing. The Scripture makes reference to gifts of healing (I Corinthians 12:9B).

Many are confused concerning this, but only because of misinterpretation. Some claim this infers that one has a gift to heal burns, another a gift for the measles, etc. No wonder physicians laugh! The truth of the matter is that every healing is a gift — every healing you or anyone else has ever received or ever will receive. But we are not studying "a" gift of healing. You may have received many of them. We are studying "the" gift of healing. This is quite a different subject.

WHAT IT IS

The gift of healing is the God-given ability to impart the healing virtue of Jesus Christ to others. Healing is a vast subject in itself, without taking thought concerning the ability to impart healing virtue.

The priests and prophets of Old Testament days ministered healing. Eli ministered to Hannah regarding her barrenness, and she was an outstanding case of deliverance and healing.

And she was in bitterness of soul, and prayed unto the LORD, and wept sore.

And she vowed a vow, and said, O LORD of hosts, if thou wilt indeed look on the affliction of thine handmaid, and remember me, and not forget thine

handmaid, but wilt give unto thine handmaid a man child, then I will give him unto the LORD all the days of his life, and there shall no razor come upon his head.

And it came to pass, as she continued praying before the LORD, that Eli marked her mouth.

Now Hannah, she spake in her heart; only her lips moved, but her voice was not heard: therefore Eli thought she had been drunken.

And Eli said unto her, How long wilt thou be drunken? Put away thy wine from thee.

And Hannah answered and said, No, my lord, I am a woman of a sorrowful spirit: I have drunk neither wine nor strong drink, but have poured out my soul before the LORD.

Count not thine handmaid for a daughter of Belial: for out of the abundance of my complaint and grief have I spoken hitherto.

Then Eli answered and said, Go in peace: and the God of Israel grant thee thy petition that thou hast asked of him.
I Samuel 1:10-17

That her petition was answered according to his word is ample manifested.

And they rose up in the morning early, and worshipped before the LORD, and returned, and came to their house to Ramah: and Elkanah knew Hannah his wife; and the LORD remembered her.

Wherefore it came to pass, when the time was come about after Hannah had conceived, that she bare a son, and called his name Samuel, saying, Because I have asked him of the LORD.
I Samuel 1:19-20

David was a miracle of healing, and he bore testimony to the fact.

I will extol thee, O LORD; for thou hast lifted me up, and hast not made my foes to rejoice over me.

O LORD my God, I cried unto thee, and thou hast healed me.

O LORD, thou hast brought up my soul from the grave: thou hast kept me alive, that I should not go down to the pit.
Psalm 30:1-3

Hezekiah was a miracle of deliverance and healing, after inspired utterance had declared that he would die!

In those days was Hezekiah sick unto death. And Isaiah the prophet the son of Amoz came unto him, and said unto him, Thus saith the LORD, Set thine house in order: for thou shalt die, and not live.

Then Hezekiah turned his face toward the wall, and prayed unto the LORD,

And said, Remember now, O LORD, I beseech thee, how I have walked before thee in truth and with a perfect heart, and have done that which is good in thy sight. And Hezekiah wept sore.

Then came the word of the LORD to Isaiah, saying,

Go, and say to Hezekiah, Thus saith the LORD, the God of David thy father, I have heard thy prayer, I have seen thy tears: behold, I will add unto thy days fifteen years.
Isaiah 38:1-5

There are many more cases of healing recorded in the Old Testament, but these few will answer our purpose well. They have been chosen because they differ so. In every case the mode employed was different; but the results were the same.

In the New Testament we read of healings in abundance under the hand and ministry of Jesus of Nazareth. He healed Peter's mother-in-law.

He arose out of the synagogue, and entered into Simon's house. And Simon's wife's mother was taken with a great fever; and they besought Him for her.

And he arose out of the synagogue, and entered into Simon's house. And Simon's wife's mother was taken with a great fever; and they besought him for her.

And he stood over her, and rebuked the fever; and it left her: and immediately she arose and ministered unto them.
Luke 4:38-39

During one of His campaigns, the sick of an entire city were healed.

And at even, when the sun did set, they brought unto him all that were diseased, and them that were possessed with devils.

And all the city was gathered together at the door.

And he healed many that were sick of divers diseases, and cast out many devils; and suffered not the devils to speak, because they knew him.
Mark 1:32-34

One particular sabbath day in the synagogue, He healed a man with a withered hand:

And it came to pass also on another sabbath, that he entered into the synagogue and taught: and there was a man whose right hand was withered.

And the scribes and Pharisees watched him, whether he would heal on the sabbath day; that they might find an accusation against him.

But he knew their thoughts, and said to the man which had the withered hand, Rise up, and stand forth in the midst. And he arose and stood forth.

Then said Jesus unto them, I will ask you one thing; Is it lawful on the sabbath days to do good, or to do evil? To save life, or to destroy it?

And looking round about upon them all, he said unto the man, Stretch forth thy hand. And he did so: and his hand was restored whole as the other.
Luke 6:6-10

One day John the Baptist (who was in the prison) sent two of his disciples to interview Jesus. When they arrived they found Him conducting an outdoor service of unheard-of proportions.

And in that same hour he cured many of their infirmities and plagues, and of evil spirits; and unto many that were blind he gave sight.
Luke 7:21

Christ's ministry of healing was such that the prophet Malachi could refer to it in the following manner:

But unto you that fear my name shall the Sun of righteousness arise with healing in his wings; and ye shall go forth, and grow up as calves of the stall.
Malachi 4:2

Other Scriptures record:

Then came the Jews round about him, and said unto him, How long dost thou make us to doubt? If thou be the Christ, tell us plainly.

Jesus answered them, I told you, and ye believed not: the works that I do in my Father's name, they bear witness of me.
John 10:24-25

Ye men of Israel, hear these words; Jesus of Nazareth, a man approved of God among you by miracles and wonders and signs, which God did by him in the midst of you, as ye yourselves also know:
Acts 2:22

136

How God anointed Jesus of Nazareth with the Holy Ghost and with power: who went about doing good, and healing all that were oppressed of the devil; for God was with him.
Acts 10:38

The prophet Isaiah declared in inspired utterance that when Christ came, mighty miracles of healing would be manifested.

Say to them that are of a fearful heart, Be strong, fear not: behold, your God will come with vengeance, even God with a recompense; he will come and save you.

Then the eyes of the blind shall be opened, and the ears of the deaf shall be unstopped.

Then shall the lame man leap as an hart, and the tongue of the dumb sing: for in the wilderness shall waters break out, and streams in the desert.
Isaiah 35:4-6

That this prophecy refers to Jesus of Nazareth is absolutely and unequivocally established.

And she shall bring forth a son, and thou shalt call his name JESUS: for he shall save his people from their sins.
Matthew 1:21

The "your God ... he will come and save you" of Isaiah's prophecy, and the "he shall save his people from their sins" of Matthew's gospel are the proof positive.

However, the foregoing inspired utterances of Isaiah and Matthew do not prove only that the Christ was the one the prophecy concerned. They also prove, beyond a shadow of a doubt, that Christ was God incarnate. This is confirmed, of course, by other Scriptures as well.

To wit, that God was in Christ, reconciling the world unto himself, not imputing their trespasses unto them; and hath committed unto us the word of reconciliation.
II Corinthians 5:19

Isaiah also foretold the virgin birth of the Saviour.

Therefore the Lord himself shall give you a sign; Behold, a virgin shall conceive, and bear a son, and shall call his name Immanuel.
Isaiah 7:14

The fact that the birth of Jesus Christ was what he was referring to, Matthew makes plain, at the same time confirming the fact that God was in Christ.

Now all this was done, that it might be fulfilled which was spoken of the Lord by the prophet, saying,

Behold, a virgin shall be with child, and shall bring forth a son, and they shall call his name Emmanuel, which being interpreted is, God with us.
Matthew 1:22-23

It is written of Jesus:

Now when the sun was setting, all they that had any sick with divers diseases brought them unto him; and he laid his hands on every one of them, and healed them.
Luke 4:40

He Himself said of His own ministry:

... Behold, I cast out devils, and I do cure...
Luke 13:32B

The ministries of the apostles and preachers of the early church were largely ministries of healing, with the gift of healing playing a very important role therein. Multitudes were healed in the streets of old Jerusalem.

Insomuch that they brought forth the sick into the streets, and laid them on beds and couches, that at the least the shadow of Peter passing by might overshadow some of them.

There came also a multitude out of the cities round about unto Jerusalem, bringing sick folks, and them which were vexed with unclean spirits: and they were healed every one.
Acts 5:15-16

In Philip's campaign in the city of Samaria, multitudes were healed.

Then Philip went down to the city of Samaria, and preached Christ unto them.

And the people with one accord gave heed unto those things which Philip spake, hearing and seeing the miracles which he did.

For unclean spirits, crying with loud voice, came out of many that were possessed with them: and many taken with palsies, and that were lame, were healed.
Acts 8:5-7

Saul of Tarsus was a miracle of healing at the very commencement of his Christian experience, under the hands of Ananias.

And Ananias went his way, and entered into the house; and putting his hands on him said, Brother Saul, the Lord, even Jesus, that appeared unto thee in the way as thou camest, hath sent me, that thou mightest receive thy sight, and be filled with the Holy Ghost.

And immediately there fell from his eyes as it had been scales: and he received sight forthwith, and arose, and was baptized.
                                                                    Acts 9:17-18

Peter healed a man sick of the palsy, at Lydda.

And it came to pass, as Peter passed throughout all quarters, he came down also to the saints which dwelt at Lydda.

And there he found a certain man named Aeneas, which had kept his bed eight years, and was sick of the palsy.

And Peter said unto him, Aeneas, Jesus Christ maketh thee whole: arise, and make thy bed. And he arose immediately.

And all that dwelt at Lydda and Saron saw him, and turned to the Lord.
                                                                    Acts 9:32-35

Paul healed a cripple at Lystra.

And there sat a certain man at Lystra, impotent in his feet, being a cripple from his mother's womb, who never had walked:

The same heard Paul speak: who steadfastly beholding him, and perceiving that he had faith to be healed,

Said with a loud voice, Stand upright on thy feet. And he leaped and walked.
                                                                    Acts 14:8-10

Publius' father was healed under the hands of Paul, and as a consequence many others on the island of Melita were healed.

In the same quarters were possessions of the chief man of the island, whose name was Publius; who received us, and lodged us three days courteously.

And it came to pass, that the father of Publius lay sick of a fever and of a bloody flux: to whom Paul entered in, and prayed, and laid his hands on him, and healed him.

So when this was done, others also, which had diseases in the island, came, and were healed:
                                                                    Acts 28:7-9

All the apostles walked in the miraclous.

And fear came upon every soul: and many wonders and signs were done by the apostles.

Acts 2:43

And by the hands of the apostles were many signs and wonders wrought among the people; (and they were all with one accord in Solomon's porch.

Acts 5:12

These all bore testimony to the truth of the message they preached. No wonder these man prayed as they did.

And now, Lord, behold their threatenings: and grant unto thy servants, that with all boldness they may speak thy word,

By stretching forth thine hand to heal; and that signs and wonders may be done by the name of thy holy child Jesus.

Acts 4:29-30

These men understood healing. They understood their ministries. They understood what the gift of healing was, and its place in their ministries and in the work and plan of God.

Properly to understand the gift of healing, one should understand thoroughly the significance of the terminology employed by our Lord when He commissioned His followers to heal the sick.

And when he had called unto him his twelve disciples, he gave them power against unclean spirits, to cast them out, and to heal all manner of sickness and all manner of disease.

Matthew 10:1

And as ye go, preach, saying, The kingdom of heaven is at hand.

Heal the sick, cleanse the lepers, raise the dead, cast out devils...

Matthew 10:7-8

Then he called his twelve disciples together, and gave them power and authority over all devils, and to cure diseases.

And he sent them to preach the kingdom of God, and to heal the sick.

Luke 9:1-2

And into whatsoever city ye enter, and they receive you, eat such things as are set before you:

And heal the sick that are therein, and say unto them, The kingdom of God is come nigh unto you.
Luke 10:8-9

TO HEAL THE SICK SIGNIFIES:

1.   TO RESTORE TO HEALTH

This implies that the one receiving healing (being ministered to) has known health at one time or another and has been robbed of the level of health once enjoyed. It also implies progression.

... they shall recover
Mark 16:18C

2.   TO CURE

This signifies a setting free, a deliverance from. To do a cure means to set free from or remove the cause of a condition nothing more, nothing less. Jesus did cures. Dr. Luke, the beloved physician, used this phrase often, specially in connection with the casting out of devils.

And in that same hour he cured many of their infirmities and plagues, and of evil spirits; and unto many that were blind he gave sight.
Luke 7:21

It is noteworthy that with reference to the healing of the sick and afflicted the eminent and godly physician utilized this term more than all the other gospel writers put together, and that he never used it other than as it applied in its true medical concept.

3.   TO MAKE SOUND

To make completely whole. This is what Peter did to the cripple at the gate. When confronted by the amazed multitude in the temple, Peter, preaching Jesus unto them, said:

And his name through faith in his name hath made this man strong, whom ye see and know: yea, the faith which is by him hath given him this perfect soundness in the presence of you all.
Acts 3:16

If we this day be examined of the good deed done to the impotent man, by what means he is made whole;

141

Be it known unto you all, and to all the people of Israel, that by the name of Jesus Christ of Nazareth, whom ye crucified, whom God raised from the dead, even by him doth this man stand here before you whole.
Acts 4:9-10

4.   TO RECONCILE

Or bring together, that which has been removed apart or severed, such as broken bones, cut or torn ligaments, tendons, tissue, etc.

It is perfectly natural for the body to recover from a malcondition, once the cause of the condition has been successfully removed. All medical men, and any others who give themselves to the alleviation of human suffering, know this to be true. That is why they strive so desperately to ascertain the causes of diversities of malconditions prevalent among people today.

It is not natural for the body to be ill. The human body, given a chance, will repair itself; something no other machine will do. If there is a reason for its illness, (and there has to be), that reason (cause) must first be removed or the body cannot recover. Men of God who do not understand this simple principle, battle blindly in the realm of healing. They do not understand that which is self-apparent; therefore there is fanaticism in this field. Anyone can see at a glance that to heal the sick demands the operation of more than the gift of healing, when you remember that the gift of healing is nothing more and nothing less than the God-given ability to impart the healing virtue of Jesus Christ. Now when we say this, please remember that it is only by the effectual working of that power which is in us.

And what is the exceeding greatness of his power to us-ward who believe, according to the working of his mighty power,

Which he wrought in Christ, when he raised him from the dead, and set him at his own right hand in the heavenly places,
Ephesians 1:19-20

When the woman with the issue of blood touched Jesus, He said:

....Somebody hath touched me: for I perceive that virtue is gone out of me.
Luke 8:46

And please note that there went virtue out of Him and healed them.

And the whole multitude sought to touch him: for there went virtue out of him, and healed them all.
Luke 6:19

142

This virtue is nothing more nor less than the life (spirit) that raised Jesus from the dead. The same verse of Scripture which declares this, declares that this same Spirit dwells in us, (the believers) and will also quicken (cause to come alive) our mortal bodies.

But if the Spirit of him that raised up Jesus from the dead dwell in you, he that raised up Christ from the dead shall also quicken your mortal bodies by his Spirit that dwelleth in you.
Romans 8:11

That this something (virtue) is the life (Spirit) of Christ, which is in us, is confirmed by the following verse:

But ye are not in the flesh, but in the Spirit, if so be that the Spirit of God dwell in you. Now if any man have not the Spirit of Christ, he is none of his.
Romans 8:9

When a person possesses and exercises the gift of healing, he simply imparts something which is in him; e.g., Peter at the temple gate.

Then Peter said, Silver and gold have I none; but such as I have give I thee: In the name of Jesus Christ of Nazareth rise up and walk.
Acts 3:6

Jesus said:

It is the spirit that quickeneth; the flesh profiteth nothing: the words that I speak unto you, they are spirit, and they are life.
John 6:63

John refers to the Spirit of God as the Spirit of life.

Paul tells us:

Now we have received, not the spirit of the world, but the spirit which is of God; that we might know the things that are freely given to us of God.
I Corinthians 2:12

The sum and substance of the foregoing is that God raised Jesus from the dead by His Spirit; that this Spirit is the resurrection life of Christ; that this life (Spirit) is the healing virtue; and that it is our privilege as God's sons to impart that Spirit, that virtue, that resurrection life of Christ, to others.

Sickness is death, in whole or in part as the case may be. Healing is life (spirit). We minister it in whole or in part as the case may require.

If we were going to speak of a ministry of healing, we would have to discuss all the gifts of the Spirit in all their diversities of operations in connection with it. We shall, in a further study. Suffice it for now, that the gift of healing is nothing more nor less than the God-given ability to impart, to pass on, the healing virtue, the resurrection life (Spirit) of Christ, to others.

Heal the sick, cleanse the lepers, raise the dead, cast out devils: freely ye have received, freely give.
Matthew 10:8

CHAPTER NINE

THE GIFT OF THE PERFORMING OF MIRACLES

Verily, verily, I say unto you, He that believeth on me, the works that I do shall he do also; and greater works than these shall he do; because I go unto my Father.

John 14:12

WHAT IT IS NOT

It is not the gift of miracles. There is no such gift. It is the gift of the performing of miracles. Let us be careful about the phraseology we employ when we refer to any of the gifts of the Spirit. Faulty phraseology here may beget false doctrine later. It is the father of much of the confusion existent today among God's people concerning spiritual gifts.

WHAT IT IS

Before we can properly declare what the gift of the performing of miracles actually is, we shall have to know what constitutes a miracle. A miracle is a supernatural act or occurrence: that which is contrary to or beyond realm of the laws of nature. The gift of the performing of miracles, therefore, is the God-given ability to perform, to cause to come to pass, acts that are supernatural, that are beyond the realm of or contrary to the laws of nature.

We see this gift in operation in the ministry of Moses as he turns his rod into a serpent and vice versa.

And Moses answered and said, But, behold, they will not believe me, nor hearken unto my voice: for they will say, The LORD hath not appeared unto thee.

And the LORD said unto him, What is that in thine hand? And he said, A rod.

And he said, Cast it on the ground. And he cast it on the ground, and it became a serpent; and Moses fled from before it.

And the LORD said unto Moses, Put forth thine hand, and take it by the tail. And he put forth his hand, and caught it, and it became a rod in his hand:

Exodus 4:1-4

And Moses and Aaron did so, as the LORD commanded; and he lifted up the rod, and smote the waters that were in the river, in the sight of Pharaoh, and in the sight of his servants; and all the waters that were in the river were turned to blood.

Exodus 7:20

145

And the LORD spake unto Moses, Say unto Aaron, Stretch forth thine hand with thy rod over the streams, over the rivers, and over the ponds, and cause frogs to come up upon the land of Egypt.

And Aaron stretched out his hand over the waters of Egypt; and the frogs came up, and covered the land of Egypt.
Exodus 8:5-6

Regarding the fact that the Lord told Moses to tell Aaron to stretch forth the rod over the water, there need be no confusion. Aaron simply stretched forth the rod (went through the motions); Moses produced the miracle. The Word of God is explicit concerning this fact. Nowhere in the Scriptures is Aaron referred to as having performed any miracles. Neither is there any record of his having been commissioned to perform any. On the other hand, Moses' commission is clear and distinct, and his miracle-working ministry is well attested to. Moreover, God commissioned Moses as a god unto Pharaoh. He then gave Aaron unto Moses as his (Moses') prophet.

And the LORD said unto Moses, See, I have made thee a god to Pharaoh: and Aaron thy brother shall be thy prophet.

Thou shalt speak all that I command thee: and Aaron thy brother shall speak unto Pharaoh, that he send the children of Israel out of his land.
Exodus 7:1-2

From this moment, until the deliverance of the Hebrews was an accomplished feat. Moses assumed the role and dignity of a supreme being whenever he was before Pharaoh. He ordered his prophet, Aaron, to do the works. Aaron complied. But we must return to Moses and his commission.

And the LORD said furthermore unto him, Put now thine hand into thy bosom. And he put his hand into his bosom: and when he took it out, behold, his hand was leprous as snow.

And he said, Put thine hand into thy bosom again. And he put his hand into his bosom again; and plucked it out of his bosom, and, behold, it was turned again as his other flesh.

And it shall come to pass, if they will not believe thee, neither hearken to the voice of the first sign, that they will believe the voice of the latter sign.

And it shall come to pass, if they will not believe also these two signs, neither hearken unto thy voice, that thou shalt take of the water of the river, and pour it upon the dry land: and the water which thou takest out of the river shall become blood upon the dry land.
Exodus 4:6-9

And the LORD said unto Moses, When thou goest to return into Egypt, see that thou do all those wonders before Pharaoh, which I have put in thine hand: but I will harden his heart, that he shall not let the people go.
Exodus 4:21

Moses wrought many more mighty miracles while he was in Egypt. Later, as they journeyed through the wilderness, he did other miracles, signs, and wonders. He sweetened the waters of Marah.

And when they came to Marah, they could not drink of the waters of Marah, for they were bitter: therefore the name of it was called Marah.

And the people murmured against Moses, saying, What shall we drink?

And he cried unto the LORD; and the LORD shewed him a tree, which when he had cast into the waters, the waters were made sweet: there he made for them a statute and an ordinance, and there he proved them,
Exodus 15:23-25

He brought forth water from the rock Horeb.

And the LORD said unto Moses, Go on before the people, and take with thee of the elders of Israel; and thy rod, wherewith thou smotest the river, take in thine hand, and go.

Behold, I will stand before thee there upon the rock in Horeb; and thou shalt smite the rock, and there shall come water out of it, that the people may drink. And Moses did so in the sight of the elders of Israel.
Exodus 17:5-6

You will have noticed that since leaving Egypt, Moses himself had literally produced the signs. No longer was he assuming the role of deity. No longer was Aaron his Prophet. For God was the God of the people, and Moses was His prophet. Obedient therefore to the word of his God, Moses produced the signs and the wonders.

After his death, his marvelous ministry received the honor of which it was worthy.

And there arose not a prophet since in Israel like unto Moses, whom the LORD knew face to face,

In all the signs and the wonders, which the LORD sent him to do in the land of Egypt to Pharaoh, and to all his servants, and to all his land,

And in all that mighty hand, and in all the great terror which Moses shewed in the sight of all Israel.
Deuteronomy 34:10-12

Before we continue, I would like to draw your attention to the fact that we are not studying miracles. We are studying the gift of the performing of miracles. Our subject matter, therefore, is chosen because it manifests the use of the gift of the performing of miracles. The declaration of the word regarding the miracle wrought in the heavens by Joshua bears repeating.

Then spake Joshua to the LORD in the day when the LORD delivered up the Amorites before the children of Israel, and he said in the sight of Israel, Sun, stand thou still upon Gibeon; and thou, Moon, in the valley of Ajalon.

And the sun stood still, and the moon stayed, until the people had avenged themselves upon their enemies. Is not this written in the book of Jasher? So the sun stood still in the midst of heaven, and hasted not to go down about a whole day.

Joshua 10:12-13

Elijah's ministry was nothing more nor less than miracles continually, as he walked in the use of this God-given ability.

And the word of the LORD came unto him, saying,

Arise, get thee to Zarephath, which belongeth to Zidon, and dwell there: behold, I have commanded a widow woman there to sustain thee.

So he arose and went to Zarephath. And when he came to the gate of the city, behold, the widow woman was there gathering of sticks: and he called to her, and said, Fetch me, I pray thee, a little water in a vessel, that I may drink.

And as she was going to fetch it, he called to her, and said, Bring me, I pray thee, a morsel of bread in thine hand.

And she said, As the LORD thy God liveth, I have not a cake, but an handful of meal in a barrel, and a little oil in a cruse: and, behold, I am gathering two sticks, that I may go in and dress it for me and my son, that we may eat it, and die.

And Elijah said unto her, Fear not; go and do as thou hast said: but make me thereof a little cake first, and bring it unto me, and after make for thee and for thy son.

For thus saith the LORD God of Israel, The barrel of meal shall not waste, neither shall the cruse of oil fail, until the day that the LORD sendeth rain upon the earth.

And she went and did according to the saying of Elijah: and she, and he, and her house, did eat many days.

And the barrel of meal wasted not, neither did the cruse of oil fail, according to the word of the LORD, which he spake by Elijah.
I Kings 17:8-16

This mighty man of God divided Jordan with his overcoat.

And Elijah took his mantle, and wrapped it together, and smote the waters, and they were divided hither and thither, so that they two went over on dry ground.
II Kings 2:8

Elijah caused the rain to cease from the earth for about three and a half years.

And Elijah the Tishbite, who was of the inhabitants of Gilead, said unto Ahab, As the LORD God of Israel liveth, before whom I stand, there shall not be dew nor rain these years, but according to my word.
I Kings 17:1

Jesus cursed a fig tree one day as He journeyed from Bethany to Jerusalem. The next day, His disciples said that the tree was dead. They drew His attention to it, and Jesus, encouraging them to have faith in God, said:

For verily I say unto you, That whosoever shall say unto this mountain, Be thou removed, and be thou cast into the sea; and shall not doubt in his heart, but shall believe that those things which he saith shall come to pass; he shall have whatsoever he saith.
Mark 11:23

Elijah, the man of God, understood this, and simply applied it to the causing of the rain to cease, etc.

Elias was a man subject to like passions as we are, and he prayed earnestly that it might not rain: and it rained not on the earth by the space of three years and six months.

And he prayed again, and the heaven gave rain, and the earth brought forth her fruit.
James 5:17-18

The fact that Elijah prayed, and prayed earnestly, about this matter does not alter the situation, as some think. He was, quite properly, praying about the situation at hand, and (there is no doubt) he received guidance from God to do and say what he said and did.

As with every outstanding man of God, he had a protégé, a disciple extraordinaire, a Timothy; and this young man's name was Elisha. He likewise

divided Jordan, using for his instrument-of-division the mantle of Elijah which he
had retrieved as the aged prophet was carried away to heaven in a whirlwind.

> And it came to pass, as they still went on, and talked, that, behold, there
> appeared a chariot of fire, and horses of fire, and parted them both asunder;
> and Elijah went up by a whirlwind into heaven.
>
> And Elisha saw it, and he cried, My father, my father, the chariot of Israel,
> and the horsemen thereof. And he saw him no more: and he took hold of his
> own clothes, and rent them in two pieces.
>
> He took up also the mantle of Elijah that fell from him, and went back, and
> stood by the bank of Jordan;
>
> And he took the mantle of Elijah that fell from him, and smote the waters, and
> said, Where is the LORD God of Elijah? And when he also had smitten the
> waters, they parted hither and thither: and Elisha went over.
> **II Kings 2:11-14**

Elisha healed the waters of Jericho.

> And the men of the city said unto Elisha, Behold, I pray thee, the situation of
> this city is pleasant, as my lord seeth: but the water is naught, and the ground
> barren.
>
> And he said, Bring me a new cruse, and put salt therein. And they brought it
> to him.
>
> And he went forth unto the spring of the waters, and cast the salt in there, and
> said, Thus saith the LORD, I have healed these waters; there shall not be from
> thence any more death or barren land.
>
> So the waters were healed unto this day, according to the saying of Elisha
> which he spake.
> **II Kings 2:19-22**

For the wife of one of the sons of the prophets, he multiplied oil.

> Now there cried a certain woman of the wives of the sons of the prophets unto
> Elisha, saying, Thy servant my husband is dead; and thou knowest that thy
> servant did fear the LORD: and the creditor is come to take unto him my two
> sons to be bondmen.
>
> And Elisha said unto her, What shall I do for thee? Tell me, what hast thou in
> the house? And she said, Thine handmaid hath not any thing in the house, save
> a pot of oil.

Then he said, Go, borrow thee vessels abroad of all thy neighbours, even empty vessels; borrow not a few.

And when thou art come in, thou shalt shut the door upon thee and upon thy sons, and shalt pour out into all those vessels, and thou shalt set aside that which is full.

So she went from him, and shut the door upon her and upon her sons, who brought the vessels to her; and she poured out.

And it came to pass, when the vessels were full, that she said unto her son, Bring me yet a vessel. And he said unto her, There is not a vessel more. And the oil stayed.

Then she came and told the man of God. And he said, Go, sell the oil, and pay thy debt, and live thou and thy children of the rest.
II Kings 4:1-7

Elisha healed poisoned food for the sons of the prophets.

And Elisha came again to Gilgal: and there was a dearth in the land; and the sons of the prophets were sitting before him: and he said unto his servant, Set on the great pot, and seethe pottage for the sons of the prophets.

And one went out into the field to gather herbs, and found a wild vine, and gathered thereof wild gourds his lap full, and came and shred them into the pot of pottage: for they knew them not.

So they poured out for the men to eat. And it came to pass, as they were eating of the pottage, that they cried out, and said, O thou man of God, there is death in the pot. And they could not eat thereof.

But he said, Then bring meal. And he cast it into the pot; and he said, Pour out for the people, that they may eat. And there was no harm in the pot.
II Kings 4:38-41

He multiplied food.

And there came a man from Baalshalisha, and brought the man of God bread of the firstfruits, twenty loaves of barley, and full ears of corn in the husk thereof. And he said, Give unto the people, that they may eat.

And his servitor said, What, should I set this before an hundred men? He said again, Give the people, that they may eat: for thus saith the LORD, They shall eat, and shall leave thereof.

So he set it before them, and they did eat, and left thereof, according to the word of the LORD.
II Kings 4:42-44

151

By the operation of the gift of the performing of miracles he caused an iron axe head to swim.

So he went with them. And when they came to Jordan, they cut down wood.

But as one was felling a beam, the axe head fell into the water: and he cried, and said, Alas, master! For it was borrowed.

And the man of God said, Where fell it? And he shewed him the place. And he cut down a stick, and cast it in thither; and the iron did swim.

Therefore said he, Take it up to thee. And he put out his hand, and took it.
II Kings 6:4-7

Jesus of Nazareth, walking in the use of all the gifts of the Spirit, had a ministry second to none in the performing of miracles. He turned water into wine.

And there were set there six waterpots of stone, after the manner of the purifying of the Jews, containing two or three firkins apiece.

Jesus saith unto them, Fill the waterpots with water. And they filled them up to the brim.

And he saith unto them, Draw out now, and bear unto the governor of the feast. And they bare it.

When the ruler of the feast had tasted the water that was made wine, and knew not whence it was: (but the servants which drew the water knew;) the governor of the feast called the bridegroom,

And saith unto him, Every man at the beginning doth set forth good wine; and when men have well drunk, then that which is worse: but thou hast kept the good wine until now.

This beginning of miracles did Jesus in Cana of Galilee, and manifested forth his glory; and his disciples believed on him.
John 2:6-11

Jesus had been preaching to the multitude. The time was far spent and He desired to feed them.

One of his disciples, Andrew, Simon Peter's brother, saith unto him,

There is a lad here, which hath five barley loaves, and two small fishes: but what are they among so many?

And Jesus said, Make the men sit down. Now there was much grass in the place. So the men sat down, in number about five thousand.

And Jesus took the loaves; and when he had given thanks, he distributed to the disciples, and the disciples to them that were set down; and likewise of the fishes as much as they would.

When they were filled, he said unto his disciples, Gather up the fragments that remain, that nothing be lost.

Therefore they gathered them together, and filled twelve baskets with the fragments of the five barley loaves, which remained over and above unto them that had eaten.
John 6:8-13

One time His disciples were caught in a boat in a storm in the midst of the sea of Galilee. Jesus came to them walking on the water.

So when they had rowed about five and twenty or thirty furlongs, they see Jesus walking on the sea, and drawing nigh unto the ship: and they were afraid.

But he saith unto them, It is I; be not afraid.
John 6:19-20

Another time He fed a multitude, this time dividing seven loaves amongst four thousand men, their wives and their children.

Then Jesus called his disciples unto him, and said, I have compassion on the multitude, because they continue with me now three days, and have nothing to eat: and I will not send them away fasting, lest they faint in the way.

And his disciples say unto him, Whence should we have so much bread in the wilderness, as to fill so great a multitude?

And Jesus saith unto them, How many loaves have ye? And they said, Seven, and a few little fishes.

And he commanded the multitude to sit down on the ground.

And he took the seven loaves and the fishes, and gave thanks, and brake them, and gave to his disciples, and the disciples to the multitude.

And they did all eat, and were filled: and they took up of the broken meat that was left seven baskets full.

And they that did eat were four thousand men, beside women and children.
Matthew 15:32-38

153

He was crossing the sea in a ship with His disciples one day when a great storm arose suddenly. He calmed the sea and the wind.

And there arose a great storm of wind, and the waves beat into the ship, so that it was now full.

And he was in the hinder part of the ship, asleep on a pillow: and they awake him, and say unto him, Master, carest thou not that we perish?

And he arose, and rebuked the wind, and said unto the sea, Peace, be still. And the wind ceased, and there was a great calm.
Mark 4:37-39

He raised Jairus' daughter from the dead. We have utilized this case previously. However, we shall study it from a different point of view. Note particularly the emphasized statements in this Scripture portion, which we set forth again for your benefit.

While he yet spake, there cometh one from the ruler of the synagogue's house, saying to him, Thy daughter is dead; trouble not the Master.

But when Jesus heard it, he answered him, saying, Fear not: believe only, and she shall be made whole.

And when he came into the house, he suffered no man to go in, save Peter, and James, and John, and the father and the mother of the maiden.

And all wept, and bewailed her: but he said, Weep not; she is not dead, but sleepeth.

And they laughed him to scorn, knowing that she was dead.

And he put them all out, and took her by the hand, and called, saying, Maid, arise.

And her spirit came again, and she arose straightway: and he commanded to give her meat.
Luke 8:49-55

As Jesus entered the city of Nain one day, He met a funeral procession. Stopping it. He raised to life the young man who was being carried on the burial, thus restoring him to his widowed mother.

And he came and touched the bier: and they that bare him stood still. And he said, Young man, I say unto thee, Arise.

And he that was dead sat up, and began to speak. And he delivered him to his mother.
Luke 7:14-15

What was perhaps the greatest of all the miracles wrought by the Lord Jesus was that of raising Lazarus of Bethany from the dead. The daughter of Jairus was dead for but a brief period of time.

The son of the widow of Nain had been dead only for a sufficient period of time to permit preparation of his body for burial (he was not yet entombed). Lazarus was dead and had been in the tomb for four days; and now Jesus stood at the mouth of that tomb (the stone having been rolled away).

And when he thus had spoken, he cried with a loud voice, Lazarus, come forth.

And he that was dead came forth, bound hand and foot with graveclothes: and his face was bound about with a napkin. Jesus saith unto them, Loose him, and let him go.
John 11:43-44

The emphasized portions of the foregoing scriptural statement of facts draws particular attention to the various miraculous aspects of this case. Note also the statement made by the priests at this time:

Then gathered the chief priests and the Pharisees a council, and said, What do we? For this man doeth many miracles.
John 11:47

As it is with many of them that preach Him today, so it was, apparently, with Christ Himself at times: the treasury was not always abundant. One day Jesus was a little short of cash for the tribute money. He sent Peter, therefore, to the sea to catch a fish.

And when they were come to Capernaum, they that received tribute money came to Peter, and said, Doth not your master pay tribute?

He saith, Yes. And when he was come into the house, Jesus prevented him, saying, What thinkest thou, Simon? Of whom do the kings of the earth take custom or tribute? Of their own children, or of strangers?

Peter saith unto him, Of strangers. Jesus saith unto him, Then are the children free.

Notwithstanding, lest we should offend them, go thou to the sea, and cast an hook, and take up the fish that first cometh up; and when thou hast opened his

155

mouth, thou shalt find a piece of money: that take, and give unto them for me and thee.
Matthew 17:24-27

Jesus gave sight to the blind beggar of Jerusalem.

And as Jesus passed by, he saw a man which was blind from his birth.

And his disciples asked him, saying, Master, who did sin, this man, or his parents, that he was born blind?

Jesus answered, Neither hath this man sinned, nor his parents: but that the works of God should be made manifest in him.

I must work the works of him that sent me, while it is day: the night cometh, when no man can work.

As long as I am in the world, I am the light of the world.

When he had thus spoken, he spat on the ground, and made clay of the spittle, and he anointed the eyes of the blind man with the clay,

And said unto him, Go, wash in the pool of Siloam, (which is by interpretation, Sent.) He went his way therefore, and washed, and came seeing.
John 9:1-7

Jesus referred to the casting out of a devil as the doing of a miracle. One of His disciples, returning from a missionary tour from some region in Palestine, said in his report:

And John answered him, saying, Master, we saw one casting out devils in thy name, and he followeth not us: and we forbad him, because he followeth not us.
But Jesus said, Forbid him not: for there is no man which shall do a miracle in my name, that can lightly speak evil of me.
Mark 9:38-39

This Scripture portion contains much more than that which is stressed at this time, and perhaps no other portion of the Word teaches more fully against bigotry amongst believers. However, I use it here to make manifest the fact that Jesus declared the casting out of an evil spirit to be the doing of a miracle.

Jesus cast out many devils.

When the even was come, they brought unto him many that were possessed with devils: and he cast out the spirits with his word, and healed all that were sick:
Matthew 8:16

156

And he healed many that were sick of divers diseases, and cast out many devils; and suffered not the devils to speak, because they knew him.
Mark 1:34

And he preached in their synagogues throughout all Galilee, and cast out devils.
Mark 1:39

On the day of Pentecost, Peter, addressing the great throng which had gathered, referred to Jesus in the following manner:

Ye men of Israel, hear these words; Jesus of Nazareth, a man approved of God among you by miracles and wonders and signs, which God did by him in the midst of you, as ye yourselves also know:
Acts 2:22

At Cornelius' house in Caesarea, Peter referred to Christ's ministry in similar vein.

How God anointed Jesus of Nazareth with the Holy Ghost and with power: who went about doing good, and healing all that were oppressed of the devil; for God was with him.
Acts 10:38

John, the author of the gospel that bears his name, wrote of Christ and His ministry:

And there are also many other things which Jesus did, the which, if they should be written every one, I suppose that even the world itself could not contain the books that should be written. Amen.
John 21:25

Peter and John did miracles also. They healed the cripple at the gate of the temple. The fact that this was a miracle of healing and that these two disciples brought it to pass, the Word of God makes very plain. The Sanhedrin, sitting in judgement concerning these men in connection with the healing of this beggar, and, very obviously desirous of punishing them for having wrought this act, were compelled by the facts of the case to make the following statement:

Saying, What shall we do to these men? For that indeed a notable miracle hath been done by them is manifest to all them that dwell in Jerusalem; and we cannot deny it.
Acts 4:16

The Scriptures give further corroboration to the fact that this was a miracle, a supernatural act.

For the man was above forty years old, on whom this miracle of healing was shewed.

Acts 4:22

Peter raised Aeneas from his bed after he had laid therein for eight years, sick of the palsy.

And it came to pass, as Peter passed throughout all quarters, he came down also to the saints which dwelt at Lydda.

And there he found a certain man named Aeneas, which had kept his bed eight years, and was sick of the palsy.

And Peter said unto him, Aeneas, Jesus Christ maketh thee whole: arise, and make thy bed. And he arose immediately.

Acts 9:32-34

If you do not think this was a miracle of healing, just try getting up out of bed after you have laid therein for eight days, never mind eight years!

Peter raised Dorcas from the dead. This was another miracle. Indeed, this was a miracle of miracles.

Now there was at Joppa a certain disciple named Tabitha, which by interpretation is called Dorcas: this woman was full of good works and almsdeeds which she did.

And it came to pass in those days, that she was sick, and died: whom when they had washed, they laid her in an upper chamber.

And forasmuch as Lydda was nigh to Joppa, and the disciples had heard that Peter was there, they sent unto him two men, desiring him that he would not delay to come to them.

Then Peter arose and went with them. When he was come, they brought him into the upper chamber: and all the widows stood by him weeping, and shewing the coats and garments which Dorcas made, while she was with them.

But Peter put them all forth, and kneeled down, and prayed; and turning him to the body said, Tabitha, arise. And she opened her eyes: and when she saw Peter, she sat up.

And he gave her his hand, and lifted her up, and when he had called the saints and widows, presented her alive.

Acts 9:36-41

The apostle Paul engaged in a miracle working ministry. Special miracles were wrought under his hands at Ephesus.

And God wrought special miracles by the hands of Paul:

So that from his body were brought unto the sick handkerchiefs or aprons, and the diseases departed from them, and the evil spirits went out of them.
Acts 19:11-12

On the island of Melita (Malta), a venomous viper fastened itself to the wrist of the aged apostle. Paul should have died within minutes from the effects of the poison. However, it had no evil effect upon him.

And when Paul had gathered a bundle of sticks, and laid them on the fire, there came a viper out of the heat, and fastened on his hand.

And when the barbarians saw the venomous beast hang on his hand, they said among themselves, No doubt this man is a murderer, whom, though he hath escaped the sea, yet vengeance suffereth not to live.

And he shook off the beast into the fire, and felt no harm.
Acts 28:3-5

He restored to life the young man who fell from the third balcony and died.

And upon the first day of the week, when the disciples came together to break bread, Paul preached unto them, ready to depart on the morrow; and continued his speech until midnight.

And there were many lights in the upper chamber, where they were gathered together.

And there sat in a window a certain young man named Eutychus, being fallen into a deep sleep: and as Paul was long preaching, he sunk down with sleep, and fell down from the third loft, and was taken up dead.

And Paul went down, and fell on him, and embracing him said, Trouble not yourselves; for his life is in him.

When he therefore was come up again, and had broken bread, and eaten, and talked a long while, even till break of day, so he departed.

And they brought the young man alive, and were not a little comforted.

Acts 20:7-12

Paul healed a man instantaneously; a man who had been crippled from birth.

And there sat a certain man at Lystra, impotent in his feet, being a cripple from his mother's womb, who never had walked:

The same heard Paul speak: who steadfastly beholding him, and perceiving that he had faith to be healed,

Said with a loud voice, Stand upright on thy feet. And he leaped and walked.
Acts 14:8-10

It is very apparent that all the apostles walked in the use of the gift of the performing of miracles.

And by the hands of the apostles were many signs and wonders wrought among the people; (and they were all with one accord in Solomon's porch.
Acts 5:12

Our God is a miracle-working God. Though He made His servants able to perform miracles, and signs, and wonders to the confirming of the message they proclaimed, He likewise bore testimony to it.

God also bearing them witness, both with signs and wonders, and with divers miracles, and gifts of the Holy Ghost, according to his own will?
Hebrews 2:4

But we have not listed among all the foregoing any of the many mighty miracles which our God wrought to confirm the ministries of our forefathers in the faith. Neither have we referred to any of the acts of creation. Our God wrought those miracles. We have not mentioned the earthquake at Philippi which He brought to pass that the Philippians might know that He was the true God, that these men were His servants and that the message they proclaimed was the truth.

We have listed only miracles wrought by men. These were chosen as examples because they were, in every case, miracles that were performed by the party specified in connection with the miracles listed.

Our reason for so doing is a very practical one. Note, we have been studying the gift of the performing of miracles, not studying miracles. There is a difference. Please remember: the gift of the performing of miracles is the God-given ability to cause to come to pass supernatural acts, acts that are contrary to or beyond the realm of the laws of nature.

Behold, I and the children whom the LORD hath given me are for signs and for wonders in Israel from the LORD of hosts, which dwelleth in mount Zion.
Isaiah 8:18

160

To contact Dr. Charles Dixon for speaking engagements, to conduct seminars or crusades, please contact him at the following:

Dr. Charles Dixon
Charles Dixon Global Ministries
P.O. Box 34533
San Antonio, TX 78265

(210) 491-0255
(210) 491-0694 fax